# PEACE EDUCATION

There is a huge volume of work on war and its causes, most of which treats its political and economic roots. In *Peace Education: How We Come to Love and Hate War*, Nel Noddings explores the psychological factors that support war: nationalism, hatred, delight in spectacles, masculinity, religious extremism, and the search for existential meaning. She argues that while schools can do little to reduce the economic and political causes of war, they can do much to moderate the psychological factors that promote violence by helping students understand the forces that manipulate them.

Nel Noddings is Lee L. Jacks Professor of Education, Emerita, at Stanford University. She is a past president of the National Academy of Education, the Philosophy of Education Society, and the John Dewey Society. In addition to 17 books – among them *Caring: A Feminine Approach to Ethics and Moral Education, Women and Evil, The Challenge to Care in Schools, Educating for Intelligent Belief or Unbelief*, and *Philosophy of Education* – she is the author of more than 200 articles and chapters on various topics ranging from the ethics of care to mathematical problem solving. Her latest books are *Happiness and Education, Educating Citizens for Global Awareness, Critical Lessons: What Our Schools Should Teach, When School Reform Goes Wrong*, and *The Maternal Factor: Two Paths of Morality*. Her work has so far been translated into twelve languages.

Noddings spent fifteen years as a teacher, administrator, and curriculum supervisor in public schools; she served as a mathematics department chairperson in New Jersey and as Director of the Laboratory Schools at the University of Chicago. At Stanford, she received the Award for Teaching Excellence three times. She also served as Associate Dean and as Acting Dean at Stanford for four years.

# Peace Education

## HOW WE COME TO LOVE AND HATE WAR

Nel Noddings

*Emerita, Stanford University*

CAMBRIDGE
UNIVERSITY PRESS

KH

CAMBRIDGE UNIVERSITY PRESS
Cambridge, New York, Melbourne, Madrid, Cape Town,
Singapore, São Paulo, Delhi, Tokyo, Mexico City

Cambridge University Press
32 Avenue of the Americas, New York, NY 10013-2473, USA

www.cambridge.org
Information on this title: www.cambridge.org/9781107658721

© Nel Noddings 2012

First published 2012

Printed in the United States of America

A catalog record for this publication is available from the British Library.

Library of Congress Cataloging in Publication data
Noddings, Nel.
Peace education : how we come to love and hate war / Nel Noddings.
      p.   cm.
Includes bibliographical references and index.
ISBN 978-0-521-19382-5 (hardback) – ISBN 978-1-107-65872-1 (paperback)
1. Peace – Study and teaching – Case studies.   I. Title.
             JZ5534.N63    2011
      303.6′6071–dc23           2011020723

ISBN 978-0-521-19382-5 Hardback
ISBN 978-1-107-65872-1 Paperback

11/26/12

*Dedicated to the memory of Sara (Sally) Ruddick*

# CONTENTS

# Introduction

How should we educate for peace? In asking that question, I do not mean to confine the discussion to work done in our schools. We are educated more broadly by the culture and subcultures in which we live. Many cultures, perhaps most of those in highly developed nations, are overtly or subtly militaristic. Their histories are organized around wars, and the virtues highly admired are often explicitly or derivatively those of the warrior. Forces in the larger culture make it difficult for schools to pursue the aim of educating for peace.

This book is an attempt to identify and deliberate on topics that should be addressed if we are serious about educating for peace. Perhaps it is more accurate to say that the book is about educating for peace *and* for war – that is, it is a discussion of what citizens should know about war and peace. The hope is that such an education will encourage more people to oppose war but, even if that does not happen, debate on the topic should be better informed.

When I started this project, I planned to give considerable space to the meaning of peace and what it means to live in peace. To my increasing astonishment, I found hundreds of books on the topic. Any appreciative reader would have to conclude that we know what it means to live in peace or, at least, that we have been generously informed on the topic again and again. Why then do we so often choose to go enthusiastically to war? That question became the center of my exploration. I do not spend much time on topics already discussed in our schools – for example, conflict resolution, cross-cultural understanding, and global citizenship – although all of these should be more widely studied.[1] Nor do I give much attention to the role of big business and other selfish interests. If people were less easily manipulated, even these powers would be less effective in maintaining a culture of war. The book's special contribution, I think, is its frank treatment of topics often neglected or treated with nationalistic bias: masculinity, patriotism, hatred, religion's frequent support of war, women's opposition to war, and war as an arena for the discovery of existential meaning. What follows is a brief introduction to each chapter. Its main purpose is to establish the book's structure and to reveal how each topic leads logically to the next.

In Chapter 1, I discuss the centrality of war in history. Despite the efforts of individuals and organizations devoted to peace, little has been done to change the culture that supports war. Students in today's schools may hear occasionally about peace movements, and they may be aware that a handful of heroic peace advocates have risked their public reputations and positions to protest against war. But the usual treatment of history and civics in our schools puts emphasis on the political and economic causes of war, its conduct, and its political effects. In some American history textbooks, the word *peace* does not even appear in the index, and the units may be organized along chronological lines from one war to the next.

In the last two decades, hope has arisen that the world's nations have reached the end of this horrific history, but that hope may be premature, and even if we have reached a point at which people reject war between nations, civil wars and other forms of organized violence continue to threaten our peace.

Chapter 2 concentrates on the destruction caused by war. Instead of presenting the cold facts about casualties, money spent, buildings destroyed, ideals upheld, and medals presented, perhaps we should spend more time telling the stories of lives disrupted, bodies mangled, nature trampled, and moral identities shattered. This last – the loss of moral identity – will be an important theme in the chapter and throughout the book. Relevant stories are widely available, but they are rarely included in the school curriculum, and when they are read, the focus is rarely on this theme. For example, most students read parts or all of the *Iliad*. That great poem tells of the destruction of bodies in gory detail, and it portrays the loss of moral identity in Achilles as he goes berserk on the field of battle, but too often teachers concentrate on the names of characters and Homer's poetic devices. Rarely are students asked to read Simone Weil's essay

"The Iliad, Poem of Might" as a vivid, horrified comment on the loss of moral control in the *Iliad*.[2]

I am certainly not the first to advocate the study of art and literature as part of peace education, and as we examine tales of destruction in Chapter 2, I will acknowledge that these efforts, from Virginia Woolf to Susan Sontag, have had little effect. Indeed, many people enjoy stories of destruction, and some even enjoy participating in the actual destruction and violence of war. J. G. Gray notes three attractions of war: "the delight of seeing [war as spectacle], the delight in comradeship, the delight in destruction."[3] This topic leads naturally to the next.

In Chapter 3, we look at what might be called the *cult of masculinity* and the warrior. What supports war? School studies emphasize the competition for resources, hatred born of cultural misunderstanding, and the struggle for power, and today's schools should be praised for introducing powerful work on multicultural understanding and conflict resolution. However, I will argue that it is also necessary to examine human nature from evolutionary and psychological perspectives. Are males violent by nature? If, as many evolutionists believe today, males have indeed inherited an evolutionary tendency to violence, why do our patterns of socialization aggravate the tendency by promoting a model of masculinity that makes the willingness and ability to fight virtues? Can this pattern of socialization be changed?

Closely related to the evolutionary tendency to male violence is the equally powerful tendency for altruism to occur along bloodlines. Humans are naturally constituted to protect those genetically related to them. Moral philosophers have often ignored this fact about human nature, supposing that clear reasoning about moral problems will allow us to make universal judgments about right and wrong. Without declaring that standing with one's own – whether they be right or wrong – is a moral principle to be followed, I will argue that any moral system that ignores our natural tendencies is likely to be ineffective in guiding moral life. None of this talk of evolutionary legacies, human nature, or natural tendencies should be taken to mean that *all* males are violent or that altruism never occurs between strangers. The obvious fact that exceptions occur fairly often should lead us to explore how we might overcome the tendencies to which we object and make the exceptions the norm.

Cultural views of masculinity have produced and sustained admiration for the warrior, and virtue ethics is heavily influenced by a long tradition of starting the discussion of virtues by describing the virtues of warriors. Some of our best-loved stories center on the exploits of warriors and the heroism and tragedy induced by war. There is a vast literature on the topic, some extolling and some condemning war. William James identified the virtues of the warrior explicitly with masculinity (or manliness) and asked whether war might be "our only bulwark against effeminacy."[4] As a confessed pacifist, he rejected this idea and sought a moral equivalent of war, but unfortunately, he inadvertently supported war by defending the notion of masculinity.

Chapter 4 looks at patriotism. Education for patriotism elevates the inclination to defend our own to the national level and to encourage admiration for the warrior. Even those who find the ethics of care too parochial in locating the origins of moral life in the maternal relation often ignore that evaluation when the discussion moves to the national level and patriotism. National self-interest is publicly and proudly defended. Indeed, hardly anyone is held in greater contempt than one who betrays his or her country for whatever reason. Even when no betrayal is involved, a declaration of world citizenship can lead to bitter disapproval, even condemnation. To overcome this, some educators and philosophers recommend educating for cosmopolitanism. How likely is it that people can be educated to think of themselves as citizens of the world first, Americans second? Can we endorse such a notion?

How does patriotism support war, and can it be redefined to sustain love of country and yet reduce its identification with the military and war? We'll consider several possibilities, including the idea of a moderated or chastened patriotism,[5] but we have to recognize the power of nationalistic patriotism and how it is exalted in story, ritual, song, prayer, poetry, and memory.

Chapter 5 examines hatred. Patriotism does not always in itself provide sufficient motivation to induce people to fight. Historically, hatred (or at least contempt) for the declared enemy has often been deliberately aroused in both military and civilian populations. It is perhaps natural for human beings to try to forget the dreadful slogans and hateful comments their country used so powerfully in past wars. I think, however, that we should remember these shameful reactions and inform our children honestly about them. Memories of past hatreds – even those long put away – should help to immunize us against future attempts to arouse hatred and contempt for possible enemies.

But not all hatreds are induced by war. Sometimes long-standing hatreds smolder and encourage war, and we need to ask what supports these hatreds and keeps them alive.

Perhaps the most difficult topic related to the psychological support of war is the role of religion in sustaining it. In Chapter 6, I make an attempt to do this. Religious institutions have not been entirely innocent of encouraging hate and war. Although the major religions often claim that they are religions of peace, history does not bear out their claims. Christianity, Islam, and Judaism all have bloody histories. Hinduism and Buddhism, too, have supported violence. From the time of Augustine, Christianity has recognized that its survival depends on, or is at least closely connected to, the well-being of the states in which it operates. Church and state have cooperated by means of elaborate rituals to maintain religiously endorsed patriotism. Today's Western democracies can generously tolerate dissent, even antiwar sentiment, by small sects, but how would they react if one of the larger Christian groups condemned their military activities? Even relatively small groups of pacifists among the larger denominations have experienced strong opposition, sometimes verging on persecution. Genuine education should include an appreciative and critical examination of the role played by religion in both advocating peace and supporting war.

Chapter 7 addresses pacifism. There is a surprisingly large literature on pacifism and peacemaking. However, little of it appears in the curriculum of our public schools. As thought on pacifism has developed, there has been a shift from absolute pacifism to modified versions such as contingent pacifism, pragmatic pacifism, relative pacifism, or conditional pacifism. What pushes peace lovers away from absolute pacifism toward one of its modifications? Are the modifications worthy of the name, or should we simply drop the word *pacifism*?

Chapter 8 considers the role of women in rejecting or supporting war. I offer a brief overview of peace movements led or strongly supported by women. Special attention is given to the contrasting styles of Virginia Woolf and Jane Addams in rejecting war. We can learn a great deal from both of them. Of the two, Woolf may have had a clearer notion of the psychological factors that encourage war.

Chapter 9 explores the connection between war and existential meaning. Both opponents and proponents of war see it tied up with questions of existential meaning. Some have claimed that war brings out the best in a nation's people: solidarity, willingness to sacrifice, courage in battle or hardship, even greater personal meaning. Others have argued that it brings out the worst in us: cruelty, hatred, a perverted pleasure in destruction, brutish behavior, and a reprehensible disregard for the property and lives of enemies.

Paul Tillich has said that we live in an age characterized by an anxiety of meaninglessness.[6] The search for meaning, conscious or unconscious, has been aggravated by the debates over the freedom of consciousness that arose in the late eighteenth and nineteenth centuries. To what degree are we free to choose our attitudes and inner commitments, and to what degree are we shaped by our environment? These are questions to which schools give too little attention, and it is not surprising that we produce citizens who are confused and easily manipulated.

On the positive side, both women and men are beginning to think more seriously about home and place as centers of existential meaning. What does it mean to make a home? What does it mean to look at one's country as a home-place and not an ideology? What does it mean to be homeless? I discuss at some length the centrality of love and care for our homes, backyards, and neighborhoods. If, as Gaston Bachelard wrote, "the house shelters daydreaming, the house protects the dreamer," must it not be a center of existential meaning?[7] Why do we not give more attention to the matters of everyday life that might help us to construct existential meaning?

Finally, in Chapter 10, I explore how far we might go in schools to educate students on the psychology of war and peace. There are powerful forces working against such a program. Drawing on recent work on critical history and the power of memory, I suggest that we must be careful to examine both the factual side of history and the affective side of human memories. We must create a climate in which dramatically different views are discussed with respect and sympathy. Critical history – the facts as nearly as we can establish them – can be used to gently reshape memory, but memory cannot be obliterated, nor should it be scorned.

A program designed to promote understanding of human attitudes toward war and peace requires conscientious preparation of the field of discussion. We Americans pride ourselves on our freedom to speak, to say what we believe. But of what use is it to speak if only those who already agree with us listen? A first step toward the abolition of war is learning to listen with respect and sympathy. Can we create a climate in which teachers are both free and competent to construct and implement such a program?

# 1

## The Centrality of War in History

There can be no doubt about the centrality of war in the history of nations. History has very nearly been equated with accounts of war. Indeed, Francis Fukuyama claimed that, with the widespread embrace of liberal democracy, war between nations has become unlikely and, with no more war, history itself would end.[1] Although minor wars and civil skirmishes will continue, the existential threat to democracy has ended. The response to this pronouncement has been varied – many denying that war has become obsolete – but the centrality of war in history has not been challenged. Samuel Huntington has warned that the next wars will be "clashes of civilizations" and their defining religions, not the traditional wars between politically defined nations.[2] And Robert Kagan has described a frightening resurgence of national interests and military competition – a "return of history."[3] For those of us who would like to define future history in terms of *peace*, these are not encouraging signs.

One might challenge Fukuyama's thesis in several ways. Huntington's clash of civilizations is a possibility. Kagan's resurgence of military nationalism is another. But the degeneration of one or more democracies is still another possibility. Liberal democracies are not always stable; we can't count on the proliferation of such democracies to guarantee the end of war. It does seem right to claim that older democracies are likely to be more stable, but this is almost a tautology.[4] And perhaps many contemporary democracies contain seeds of discontent comparable to those that made Germany susceptible to Nazism. But, of course, it was *war* – World War I and the oppressive peace that followed it – that tipped the balance and opened the political door to Hitler. War begets war. With all the explanations, it is still baffling and chilling to think how a nation so advanced in literature, philosophy, art, music, religious thought, and industry could accept National Socialism. But it is clear that fledgling democracies can be derailed by tragic occurrences.

Even well-established democracies can be badly shaken by violence, especially the organized violence of war. War undermines democracy, and a weakened democracy makes further war more likely. In the United States, for example, war has often threatened democratic processes. In the Civil War, habeas corpus was frequently denied, federal forces occupied telegraph offices, and they were frequently called upon to restore civil order. The murder of blacks in the South often went unpunished, and draft riots disrupted the North. In World War I, the Espionage and Sedition Acts prescribed punishment for speech that was disloyal to the government or against the war. There was widespread abuse of German American citizens, and some orchestras even refused to play the music of Brahms, Beethoven, and Mozart. Internment of Japanese Americans in World War II was a shocking violation of civil rights, and the atomic bombings of Hiroshima and Nagasaki raised serious questions about the possibility of waging war according to principles that forbid deliberate attack on civilians. In the cold war, loyalty tests and oaths were widely applied; the McCarran Act, making it a crime to promote dictatorial forms of government, was passed over President Harry Truman's veto, and McCarthyism caused havoc in the entertainment industry. After the terrorist attacks in 2001, the government used illegal wiretaps and highly questionable methods of retaining and interrogating prisoners. So far, our democracy has held up. It is hard to say, however, what might happen in this well-established liberal democracy if terrorist attacks were to become more frequent and widespread.

There is another reason to doubt the end of war. It does seem true that stable democracies will not wage war against one another, but they frequently find reasons – justified or unjustified – to attack others. Although nuclear weapons have not been used since 1945, it hardly seems right to say that the conduct of war by the democracies has been restrained. Robert O'Connell, for example, writes that the United States exhibited "halfhearted belligerency" in Korea and Vietnam:

> In both Korea and Vietnam the United States' unwillingness to apply sufficient force to achieve victory can be traced to concerns

about provoking general war.... So the urge to be perceived as prudent and always allowing our adversaries acceptable alternatives to all-out war came to outweigh the pursuit of victory.[5]

The "restraint" exercised by the United States in Korea and Vietnam nevertheless culminated in 5 million deaths. The claim made by O'Connell and others that war has become obsolete does not seem justified.[6] Indeed, one might argue – with considerable evidence to back the contention – that the liberal democracies have found more and more effective ways to reduce their own military casualties at the expense of civilian populations in the areas of military action.

The centrality of war is underscored by a consideration of who figures in our historical accounts. In the United States, presidents who fought in or presided over wars tower over all others, and nations successful in conquest and empire building dominate world history. Clark Wissler comments on the lack of celebrated heroes among the Pueblo Indians:

> Wars seem necessary to reveal such greatness. Had the Pueblos terrorized the settlements, massacred women and children, left a trail of blood and destruction behind them, they would hold a high place in history, as we know it.[7]

Much recent work has concentrated on the origin and causes of war, and attention has been drawn to the role of agriculture and settled communities in giving birth to both nations and war. Protection of property, the drawing of boundaries, and the establishment of forts and military bases are all related. On these accounts, war – like agriculture – is a relatively recent phenomenon. But, beyond armed conflict between nations, war may be defined as organized violence, and violence has always been part of human life. If the inclination to violence is somehow built into humans, then it makes sense to look for origins in our evolutionary ancestors.[8] Understanding that biological legacy may help us to create educational theories and practices to counteract it. Ignoring it will perpetuate attempts to find the political and economic causes of war – and these efforts are certainly worthwhile – but they will not explain why war has been *central*, so widely embraced, in human history.

Both philosophy and religion have supported war. In classical philosophy, the dominant view was that war is a part of nature and, moreover, it is the engine of a state's or nation's success. This view persisted for centuries. On this account, empires are built on victories in war, and the "manliness" of a society is judged by the courage and stamina of its military. Christianity encouraged this attitude by teaching that, while peace should be the ultimate aim, it is to be achieved by the sorts of wars that would bring all peoples under the banner of Christianity. I'll say more about this in the chapter on religion.

War has long been central not only in history, philosophy, and religion, but in recreation as well. Sports are staged like battles, and huge audiences look forward to the violence of football, soccer, and boxing – while expressing dismay when a player suffers actual damage. Sometimes the violence flows over into the audience, and fights break out in the stands. In the realm of entertainment, many of us enjoy stories, films, and plays depicting battles and wars. Modern technology has made it possible to produce convincing scenes of gore and terror without actually hurting anyone; even the horses live through horrendous battles between cavalry and Indians on the western frontier. And people love these scenes. I confess to liking the moral clarity in old westerns. The good guys are really good, and the bad guys are clearly bad; we cheer when the bad guys bite the dust. Children's toys are often replicas of weapons, adult men indulge in paintball battles, and audiences gather to watch re-creations of old battles. War and warlike activities are pervasive in American life. We are led to ask why ordinary peacetime life is so boring. Must it be?

In virtually all wars, young men – some at least – join the military and experience an initial thrill at being part of a heroic enterprise. The atmosphere before the actual fighting begins is loaded with excitement: flying banners, snappy uniforms, martial music, cheering crowds, the incomparable sense of belonging to something bigger than oneself, being part of history. Remember the scenes from *Gone with the Wind* in which young southerners set out to do battle at Bull Run and their families are prepared to watch while picnicking? The odd thing is that no matter how much we learn about the horror of war, there are always people eager to be part of it, at least until they have actually experienced it. And, as we'll see, there are some who come to hate war while they are in actual combat and then, in later years, fall into a wistful idealization of the war they once hated. Other young men will pay the price of this dreamlike forgetting.

Enthusiasm for and fascination with war mix with fear and dread in the human psyche. If, as seems to be the case, humans have evolutionary inclinations to both violence and the protection of those closest to them, it should be possible to create and maintain patterns of socialization inimical to war and violence. But, as we will see in the following chapters, cultural expectations and socialization have been designed to promote pride in fighting. Can this be changed?

The possibilities are rich. In addition to encouraging critical thinking on patriotism, masculinity (and femininity), religion, the psychology of war, and love of place and home, there are many other histories that might displace war from the center. How about the history of food, of childhood, homes, sanitation, transportation, machinery, of art, music, mathematics, and religion?

The world is presently plagued by substantial wars, terrorist attacks, ethnic skirmishes, and genocide. Too often we judge the importance of such organized violence on the basis of who is suffering. If it is not our people and if the sufferers are held to be responsible for the violence, we tend to downplay the number of their casualties or find it difficult even to keep track of them. When others differ from us in religion, for example, our sympathies may be dulled, and we may feel justified in becoming aggressors. Monotheism has contributed to the legacy of self-righteous violence, and war will probably remain central in human history so long as the great monotheistic faiths exercise control over large populations.[9] We will say much more about this theme in the chapter on religion.

### THE VOCABULARY OF WAR

The vocabulary of war, even more than war itself, is central to human experience. The peace of which many of us write and speak is too often defined merely as the cessation of war.[10] Can there be peace, then, if there is no war? And how should we define *peace*? In the preface to *Women, Militarism, and War*, the editors point out that an unjust peace can be as brutal and devastating as war.[11] Thus, I would point out again that we need to get at the roots not just of war but of *violence*. A "peace" that does violence to people, nonhuman animals, or the environment is not peace as we envision it, although it may be recognized as the cessation of war. Somehow, we must create a vision of peace that does not depend on war.[12] Before we can do that, however, we have to understand why people are so attracted to war. In this book, I try to analyze and describe what we should understand about out attitudes to war and peace.

War is evaluated in an oddly ambivalent way. On the one hand, we say that we dread it, and our leaders claim that no one wants war. On the other hand, we invoke the word *war* to emphasize seriousness of purpose. We have launched wars on drugs, on poverty, and on terrorism. War, for all of its horrors, takes on a positive connotation when it is conducted against some perceived evil.

Postmodern writers and deconstructionists have said quite a lot about language and violence. They too note the ambivalence in our attitudes and claims. Discourse and violence are sometimes taken to be mutually exclusive, sometimes as mutually constitutive.[13] Those who hold that they are mutually exclusive argue that discourse and dialogue should be used to settle conflicts and avoid violence. But deconstructionists make a good point when they note that the Western language of rights and justice becomes a form of violence when it is imposed on other cultures. I would add to this by noting that talk of *rights, equality, freedom*, and *justice* is often used as justification for fighting. Such talk has become enshrined in Western politics, and it supports the practice of patriotism. Over and over again, it is proclaimed that there are values – rights, equality, freedom, justice – worth fighting for. It is rarely suggested that these things are worth *not* fighting for; that is, that they are so important that we should find nonviolent ways of protecting and promoting them. At bottom, as nations have developed and used language, it seems that discourse and violence are, as postmodern thinkers have said, often mutually constitutive.

That said, I believe deconstructionists have gone too far in identifying language with violence. The idea that "naming is violence" is almost a mantra among poststructuralists. Naming, it is said, creates an Other with all the attendant dangers in that label. But, surely, naming can also be a recognition of relation, and that recognition may effectively forbid and prevent violence. Consider a new mother, still sweating from the pain of labor, as she lays a gentle hand on the head of her infant and says, "My little darling." This is no violence; it is a pledge of lifelong love. And the understanding that other women all over the world – Others however named – speak similar words, have similar feelings and commitment should lead her to despise violence.

It might be argued that below the surface of that commitment to love is a quiet threat that the little darling will be protected if need be with violence. Yes, but it is unlikely. Females, recognizing their own limited physical capacity, are more likely to flee from aggressors or appease them than to use violence against them. In an important sense, the mutually constitutive relation of language and violence is a male construction.

It is worth spending a bit more time on the philosophers' evaluation of naming. According to Derrida, naming is an act of "originary violence."[14] But, like many philosophers, Derrida has ignored or skipped over the elements of human life, its basic biological and psychological features. *Birth* is the original violence we all go through. The good mother's first naming, whether voiced aloud or expressed through a gentle hand, makes a commitment to protect the infant from violence. It sets up the first opposition between caring relations and violence. The philosophers' neglect of real, bodily life – a neglect we will encounter repeatedly – was noted by Sara Ruddick in her discussion of philosophy and birth: "Although we are a species that knows its own natality, in philosophical texts we are 'thrown' into the universe somehow, appearing at the earliest when we can talk and read."[15]

There is another useful way of looking at speech that may do violence and speech that creates or maintains relation. Martin Buber describes the difference between saying Thou and saying It: "The world of experience belongs to the basic word I-It. The basic word I-Thou establishes the world of relation."[16] (For Buber, "experience" refers to knowing and using.) Buber notes that we cannot live entirely in a world of I-Thou; we must learn, categorize, know, use, and accomplish things. But the tragedy, he writes, is that we *can* live entirely in the world of I-It. It is this possibility that the mother forecloses when she says, "My little darling," a naming that sustains the world of relation.

The language of war is often transposed in a way that disguises or minimizes violence. We do not usually identify military life – aside from the officer corps – with the most successful or admirable way of life. In our contemporary society, it is often the youngsters who have had problems in school who enter the military right out of high school. Sometimes their parents even say, "It will make a man out of him."[17] Our attitude is very like that described more than a century ago by Rudyard Kipling in his poem "Tommy":

> For it's Tommy this, an' Tommy that, an' "Chuck him out, the brute!" /
> But it's "Saviour of 'is country" when the guns begin to shoot.[18]

So it is during today's wars. In wartime, one speaks reverentially of "our boys," "our heroes," and the nobility of their mission. It is almost impossible to draw attention to the hypocrisy involved in this language switch without being accused of antipatriotism. We'll say much more about this in the chapter on patriotism.

It is worth noting that celebratory language is rarely applied to the military in today's Germany. Indeed, many young people in German military service feel that they are looked down upon. Although this is somewhat dispiriting for those young people, it is a sign of Germany's commitment to relative pacifism. Today's Germany is resolved that there will be no more glorification of soldiers and war.

Language and violence again become mutually constitutive in the establishment of war memorials. Art and language are often beautifully combined to memorialize those who died in past wars. Monuments set in lovely landscapes bring apparent order and peace to past events that were chaotic and violent. Poetry, too, sometimes contributes to the project. Rupert Brooke, for example, anticipated his own death in battle: "If I should die, think only this of me:/ that there's some corner of a foreign field/ That is for ever England" and he finishes the poem with reference to "hearts at peace, under an English heaven."[19] If Brooke had not been killed so early in World War I, his language, like that of Wilfred Owen, might have been more reflective of war's actual horror.[20]

War memorials are offered not only as tributes to the dead but also as consolation to the living. The Great Stone at the center of the Somme memorial has this inscription: "Their name liveth for evermore." The memorial contains 73,077 names, the names of young men who were robbed of life. Note that we often say that they *gave* their lives, but of course, this is not true; their lives were taken from them. It is not outrageous to consider the carving of their names and the false promise of "evermore" another act of violence.

The collaboration of memorials and violence is pervasive. Maya Lin, designer of the Vietnam Veterans Memorial, intended her work to offer consolation – acceptance of death and recognition of mourning – and it no doubt has had this effect on many viewers. But James Tatum has described the effects of a replica of the Memorial, the Moving Wall, while it was at Norwich University, a private military academy in Vermont. The Moving Wall, like the original, provides a powerful emotional experience. While in residence at Norwich, the Wall was guarded constantly by uniformed cadets and decorated with flags. As Tatum points out: "Maya Lin's design is made to mean the opposite of what she had envisioned; mourning the dead of one war

becomes training for cadets who will fight the next."[21] Like the poetry
intended to comfort mourners and perhaps induce a commitment to
reject war, memorials contribute to its renewal.

I want to mention one other aspect of the connection between language and war, although I'm not sure what to make of it. People in the
military use language frowned upon in polite society. For many young
people just out of high school, the freedom to use bad language may
be appealing. Certainly, accounts of military conversation are loaded
with forbidden words. *Fuck*, it seems, appears in almost every military
utterance.[22] A chapter in Dexter Filkins's book on the Iraq war is entitled "Fuck Us."[23] It may be that, when events are moving rapidly, there
is no time for complete, grammatical sentences. But the language persists in barracks and recreational settings. Could the easy use of rough
language be an attempt to present the speakers as "real men"? Or, more
seriously, might the violation of socially acceptable use of language be
a sign that the entire structure of social-moral life has been cast into
question? This is a possibility we will explore in later chapters.

WAR THEORY

War has a central place not only in human history but also in thinking, in creating theories. As we've noted, war plays a prominent role
in philosophy, religion, literature, poetry, and art, and it is supported
by martial music, colorful uniforms, flags, rituals, and prayer. It is also
embedded in international law and in the language of morality.

In writing about just war theory, Michael Walzer points out the
similarity between the language of international law and the language
we ordinarily use in discussing morality. His analysis concentrates
on moral law, not on legal or military handbooks: "When I talk of
law, I am referring to the moral law, to those general principles that
we commonly acknowledge, even when we can't or won't live up
to them."[24] This statement raises an immediate question: What are
these "general principles," and to what degree are they "commonly
acknowledged"? It may be that ordinary morality and military morality differ importantly. But let's put that aside for the moment.

Walzer argues that war is a rule-governed activity and therefore can
be studied and judged from a moral perspective. He starts his analysis
by attacking the doctrine of *realism* – a doctrine that describes war as
an activity outside the realm of morality. In war, realism warns, there

is no morality. The morality "commonly acknowledged" breaks down. My position in this book is close to realism. I do not claim that there are no moral acts in war or that no one can be asked to accept responsibility for what he or she does, but I do claim that going to war is always morally questionable and that conducting war morally is realistically impossible. This is not to say that defending oneself or one's nation is immoral in itself, but the decision to mount a violent defense is fraught with immoral possibilities. It is not to say, either, that we can find no morally heroic acts in war; we can. But it is to say that every war has produced dramatically immoral acts, many of which are excused, if not justified, by the perpetrators. Because it invites such horrors and because it so often destroys the moral identity of combatants, war must be regarded as an immoral enterprise or at best as an enterprise representative of a wholly different moral domain.

Consider the two very different moral domains. In the domain of "commonly acknowledged" principles, it is wrong to kill except in immediate self-defense; in the morality of war, it is one's duty to kill those identified as enemies. In ordinary morality, it is wrong to steal; in war morality, one may steal food and appropriate property if one's leaders order or allow it. In the first domain, it is wrong to lie or bear false witness; in the second, one would certainly not tell the enemy the truth, and one is almost bound to believe a host of falsehoods about the enemy and act on them. The focus of moral devotion moves from ordinary morality to one that is governed by entirely different rules and enforced by authority that cannot be questioned. To question it is in itself morally questionable and even punishable. In addition, important forces act to support both domains. Religions, for example, have been consistent in giving contrary messages. On the one hand, they are "for peace"; on the other, since the days of Augustine, when it became clear that their survival depended on collaboration with the state, churches supported the war efforts of their nations. Young people serving in the military must somehow believe that the two moralities are not in conflict.

It is important to understand my objective in writing this book. I do not expect to create a way to eliminate war or to construct a theory of nonviolent conflict resolution, welcome as they would be, and I agree with Walzer that nonviolent resistance to aggression will rarely reduce the violence of aggressors. Gandhi was wrong on this.[25] Jewish nonviolent resistance to the Nazis would only have facilitated the genocide. Rather, I intend to explore how we can help young people to understand the psychology of war, how easily they can be swept into it, and what sustains the war mentality in our culture. With deeper understanding across a wider segment of the population, war might become genuinely unpopular. A move in this direction will not eliminate war, but it might well reduce its occurrence. Walzer's gallant attempt to get soldiers to follow the rules of war will almost certainly not work. When he writes at the end of his book that "the restraint of war is the beginning of peace,"[26] he is deceiving himself. The statement is not untrue. Such restraint in war, if exercised, might indeed be the beginning of peace, but it is unrealistic to suppose that restraint will be exercised.

Just war theory is part of what must be understood in a study of war. It has two aspects: *jus ad bellum*, a just cause for going to war, and *jus in bello*, the just conduct of war. Often both sides insist on the justice of their cause, and only outsiders can offer a defensible judgment on *jus ad bellum*. Even when one nation invades another and thereby gives the invaded nation a just cause to declare war in its defense, it is possible that a succession of severe provocations preceded the invasion. Still, it seems basically right to say that overt attack provides a just cause for the attacked group to go to war. However, the problem is further aggravated by the current use of the concept of *preventive war*, the morally questionable idea that one nation is justified in attacking another because the nation under attack represents a possible threat to the attacker and its allies. Judgment is divided on this, and students should hear the arguments on both sides.

Major problems arise in the second area. Can a war, however justified initially, be waged justly? The answer to this, from any variant of realism, is no; there will be questionable acts, horrible acts, morally unjustifiable acts on both sides. Some thinkers writing from the perspective of realism deplore these acts but accept them as a natural consequence of war and refuse to pass moral judgment on them. At that point, I part company with realism. The acts must be uncovered and assessed. But the great moral fault lies with war itself. It creates the conditions under which normally moral people commit immoral acts.

In contrast to Walzer, who, following international law, recognizes the moral equality of lawful combatants, Jeff McMahan recommends that combatants who fight for the side deemed unjust should be held morally accountable for that decision.[27] Unjust combatants are, according to McMahan, *not* morally equal to just combatants. He acknowledges that there is no feasible way of enacting a requirement that combatants be held responsible for their participation in an unjust war, but he still insists that they are, with some exceptions, morally responsible.

McMahan's arguments, well organized and expressed, present another example of the articulate philosopher moving too far away from reality. Young people who enter the military rarely have the sophistication or even the interest to read such philosophical arguments. I agree with him, however, that the matter is important, and the topic should be discussed in our schools so that students might at least become aware that a personal moral problem exists. My emphasis throughout this book is on disclosure, open dialogue, and continued exploration of all sides of the issues involving war.

Although we cannot act on McMahan's argument – and we'll see many reasons why we cannot – there are people who have voluntarily accepted it. In World War II, for example, the poet Robert Lowell refused induction into the military and explained his position in a "Declaration of Personal Responsibility" sent to the president. Lowell accepted as a fact that the United States entered the war for a just cause, but he criticized bombing raids and other attacks on civilians; he believed that the war was being conducted unjustly:

> I have come to the conclusion that I cannot participate in a war whose prosecution, as far as I can judge, constitutes a betrayal of my country.[28]

Lowell would win moral approval from McMahan, but the United States was not then following the mode of ordinary morality. We were already in full-blown war morality. Lowell was sentenced to prison and served several months of the sentence.

There is more to the problem than ignorance. Both McMahan and Walzer assume that people share "commonly acknowledged" moral principles, but they do not consider the scope of general agreement. In everyday life, people do seem to share such principles. However, a severe change in emphasis occurs in times of war, particularly among military personnel. Virtually all soldiers agree that they should not murder, steal, rape, or lie without justification in civilian life or in those facets of military life over which they have control. But many will take their pledge of loyalty and obedience to authority very seriously, and their training will enforce this obedient loyalty. The basic military code of authority, augmented by a deeply ingrained patriotism, will become their shared morality, and this new morality will displace that of previously acknowledged principles. There are, of course, those who enjoy the opportunity to flout their earlier ordinary morality, but they are not the ones who concern us here.[29] Rather, my concern is with the highly responsible young people who will, sometimes in moral agony, adopt the guiding motto, "My country right or wrong," and firmly believe that they are right in doing so. This attitude extends beyond the military to a large part of the civilian population. McMahan discusses the case of Paul Tibbets, pilot of the plane – *Enola Gay*, named for his mother – that dropped the nuclear bomb on Hiroshima.[30] On McMahan's criteria of moral responsibility, Tibbets should surely be labeled a war criminal. Yet in a wide circle of Americans, he is regarded as a hero. Cases like this illustrate the competing moralities that must be taken into account.

McMahan also puts aside the possibility of diminished capacity too easily, writing, "There are very few cases in which a soldier is wholly lacking in the capacity for morally responsible deliberation and agency."[31] Many historians, psychiatrists, and biographers tell a different story.[32] At least some cases of posttraumatic stress result from horrible things soldiers have done, not only from horrors they have undergone. These events are well documented but rarely discussed while a war is being waged. In the midst of war, as noted before, language changes: Disorderly young men become heroes overnight, questionable acts are excused or even praised, and acts that may cause a lifetime of moral pain are passed over in silence.

War and warlike activities have long been central in human life, and our attitudes toward war are characteristically ambivalent. We say that we hate it, but obviously there is a sense in which we love it. That ambivalence will be noted in every chapter that follows. We'll look next at the destruction caused by war. Certainly we deplore that destruction but, it turns out, we also love it.

# 2

# Destruction

War is enormously destructive. It destroys lives, bodies, buildings, and property. It damages the natural environment, and often it destroys or badly damages the moral identity of those who serve in the armed forces. In the previous century and a half, because war was not fought within the boundaries of the United States, it may be especially hard for young Americans to grasp the enormity of war's destruction. In this chapter, I'll look first at the destruction of lives and bodies, then in turn at the destruction of property, the natural environment, and moral identity.

## BODIES AND LIVES

It is not necessary to memorize the number of casualties in the wars of the twentieth century, but students should spend some time thinking about those numbers. In that bloody century, more than 86 million people died in wars. The terrorist attack of 9/11/01 that killed almost 3,000 was a great shock to Americans. Imagine, then, what it must be like to live under frequent bombings and see your whole neighborhood reduced to rubble. Can the bombing of civilians be defended? Just war theory and modern war conventions state that noncombatants may not be deliberately attacked, and yet the escalation of civilian deaths in twentieth-century wars was dramatic: "In World War I, 95 percent of those killed in war were soldiers, 5% were civilians; in World War II, 52 percent were soldiers, 48% civilians; in the Korean War, 16 percent were soldiers, 84% were civilians."[1] We can provide a little math problem for our students: If there were 2 million deaths in the Vietnam War and 58,000 were American soldiers, how many people did the

Vietnamese lose? And we can follow that with a social/historical question: Why is it so hard to separate the Vietnamese casualties into military and civilian? In the recent wars in Iraq and Afghanistan, civilian deaths have far outweighed those of the military.

When we spend some time considering the number of casualties, we are led to ask whose life matters. In all wars, we grieve over the deaths of our own soldiers, but the loss of enemy soldiers is often taken as something to brag about, a factor in achieving victory. In the Vietnam War, army units were awarded medals on the basis of body counts. To keep them from falling back into everyday morality, combat soldiers have long been encouraged to give disparaging names to their enemies: the Germans were "krauts" or "Huns" in World War I, the Japanese "dirty little Japs" in World War II, the North Koreans and Vietnamese "gooks," the Iraqis "ragheads." Thus is the enemy dehumanized. We'll say much more about methods of arousing and maintaining hatred and contempt in Chapter 5.

But demeaning language and the pursuit of victory do not immunize all men against human sympathy. In the Iraq war, outside Baghdad, marines fired on a minibus that failed to stop at a roadblock. The bus held a family of ten, six of whom were killed outright. Dexter Filkins, telling the story, writes:

> The marines had been keeping up a strong front when I arrived, trying to stay business-like about the incident. "Better them than us," one of them said. The marines volunteered to help lift the bodies onto a flatbed truck. One of the dead had already been partially buried, so the young marines helped dig up the corpse and lift it onto the vehicle. Then one of the marines began to cry.[2]

The young marine was caught between two contradictory moral worlds. On the one hand, "better them than us"; on the other, why should ordinary, innocent families die? What have I done? Will the young man ever get over it? It is obvious that the survivors of the Iraqi family will never get over it.

Jonathan Shay gives an account from the Vietnam War in which American soldiers, believing enemy soldiers were unloading weapons from a boat in the bay, opened fire and kept firing: "Daylight came [long pause], and we found out we killed a lot of fishermen and kids." The soldier who told the story felt betrayed by a commanding officer who treated the incident as something to be proud of:

They wanted to give us a fucking Unit Citation – them fucking maggots. A lot of medals came down from it. The lieutenants got medals, and I know the colonel got his fucking medal. And they would have award ceremonies, y'know, I'd be standing like a fucking jerk and they'd be handing out fucking medals for killing civilians.[3]

These are stories of young men torn between the emotions that govern everyday morality and the instrumental attitudes that accompany war. In war, soldiers dare not think much about the suffering of their enemies or those who, even by accident, may be associated with them. At the extreme, our religious histories and myths excuse the most atrocious conduct of those associated with "our side." Consider the Hebrew treatment of Amalekites, Canaanites, Amorites, and Moabites. Consider also the genocidal act of Yahweh in killing all of the Egyptian firstborns. This dreadful act would convince Pharaoh to let the Israelites leave Egypt. But what did Pharaoh's acts and attitudes have to do with a young mother just experiencing the miracle of birth? Why should she lose her child? Or with elderly parents dependent on their loving firstborn son? Or with a cow in the pasture with her firstborn calf? Time passes, and the outrageous suffering of one age becomes a celebration for some in another. Passover refers both to the Angel of Death "passing over" carefully marked Hebrew dwellings and to the following exodus or passing over of Hebrews out of Egypt. It seems right to celebrate the second but coldhearted to celebrate the first.

The strategy of blaming whole peoples for the crimes of their leaders is still regularly used. In World War II, many British citizens expressed the opinion that the bombing of German civilians was justified because of Hitler's unconscionable acts – the Germans "had it coming to them." Similarly, many Americans believed that the Japanese had brought the bombing of their cities on themselves. Somehow we have not yet come to understand that ordinary early Egyptians were not responsible for the acts of their pharaoh, German children for the sins of Hitler, or Japanese homemakers for the attack on Pearl Harbor.

God's purpose in causing the plague now celebrated as Passover was to mark a separation between Egyptians and Israelites, and such separations have given generations of human beings reason to fight one another. "They are not like us" helps to harden hearts and put everyday morality aside.

But sometimes human beings are led to fight people very like themselves. The American Civil War is such a case, and its casualties were enormous:

> The number of soldiers who died between 1861 and 1865, an estimated 620,000, is approximately equal to the total American fatalities in the Revolution, the War of 1812, the Mexican War, the Spanish-American War, World War I, World War II, and the Korean War combined.[4]

Civilians, too – especially in the South – died, sometimes by guerrilla violence, sometimes by starvation. Yet, the North and South were much alike in race, religion, and language. What separated them was a way of life and, in the South, a kind of local loyalty that curled up tightly around itself.

In the absence of differences that have fueled so many foreign wars, what kept America's most destructive war going? Religion played a role. Drew Gilpin Faust comments:

> Some historians have argued that, in fact, only the widespread existence of such beliefs [in immortality] made acceptance of the Civil War death tolls possible, and that religion thus in some sense enabled the slaughter.[5]

Certainly it was a time of religious ferment. Many Americans were evangelicals and attended church regularly. The presence of so much death turned others to forms of spiritualism, and séances were quite popular. At the same time, there was increasing religious skepticism promoted by transcendentalists and excited speculation on evolution. As is true even today, strongly opposing views seem to strengthen each other. Many soldiers fortified themselves with the belief, endorsed by enthusiastic preachers, that, in dying, they would begin new, better lives.

We'll give much more attention to the influence of religion on war in a later chapter, but here we should note that its effects have not been consistent. I think the weight of evidence backs the historians who argue that religion has often supported or enabled slaughter, but there are outstanding cases of individual clergymen opposing war and, of course, there are religious denominations that have adopted pacifism and worked conscientiously for peace.

In any case, religious acceptance of death does not explain the enthusiasm that sometimes accompanied the killing:

A Texas officer exulted as the enemy fell before him, "Oh this is fun to lie here and shoot them down." To a Union soldier near Harrison's Landing, Virginia, in 1862, battle "seemed like play for we would be laughing and talking to each other yelling and firing away. One fellow would say 'Watch me pop that fellow'. Another fellow said, 'I dropped a six foot sesech.'"[6]

There was something operating in the psyche of Civil War soldiers and veterans that is hard to understand today. Oliver Wendell Holmes, Jr., went to war initially with a profound moral conviction against slavery. After participating in some of the war's bloodiest battles and being wounded three times, he came to hate both war and certitude. He despised men whose certitude was used to drive other men to kill. He lost his belief in beliefs. And yet, many years later, in his "Soldier's Faith" speech on Memorial Day 1895, he said:

> War when you are at it is horrible and dull, it is only when time has passed that you see that its message was divine.... I do not doubt ... that the faith is true and adorable which leads a soldier to throw away his life in obedience to a blindly accepted duty, in a cause which he little understands, in a plan of campaign of which he has no notion, under tactics of which he does not see the use.[7]

Such talk is enigmatic. Holmes did not believe in blind obedience, certitude, or God. Why then did he glorify the dutiful soldier and war? Perhaps the duty of remembrance – so many of his friends had died dutifully – prompted him to talk this way. Or perhaps the thoughts were a throwback to the Greek idea that it is sweet and seemly to die for one's country. Or it may be a symptom of a common human longing to find meaning in past events that were essentially meaningless.

The attitude expressed by Holmes in the "Soldier's Faith" speech is heard years later in Yeats's denunciation of the World War I poet Wilfred Owen. As a great poet, Yeats certainly had the standing to criticize Owen's poetry *as poetry*, but his anger seems more to have been directed at Owen's indignation and disgust with war. That anger often seems to appear in older men (Yeats was more than sixty when he criticized Owen) whose vision of the past has been challenged. Lorrie Goldensohn remarks:

> There is surely something grotesque here about Yeats's fanatic acceptance of war's necessity, with all its attendant cruelty. In his

ancient, glittering eyes, any bitching about getting killed for no discernible cause seems to miss the point: dying heroically and uncomplainingly is all the point, since war exists perpetually. Dying is a soldier's job.[8]

Religion, regionalism, masculinity, and the urge for excitement will all be considered as we attempt to understand why human beings have willingly slaughtered one another in war after war.

In addition to millions of dead, war causes even more millions of maimed and wounded. During and after war, the suffering of the wounded and their caretakers goes on and on. In the Vietnam War there were 365,000 wounded, and the suicide rate among Vietnam veterans has been high. Moreover, many veterans are still being treated for posttraumatic stress disorder, and some may never recover.[9]

Today strategists still argue over the morality of the attacks on civilians in World War II. Piles of competing numbers furnish the data to argue over. Some insist that the bombings of Hiroshima and Nagasaki actually saved lives by bringing the Pacific war to an end. Others argue that, given the number of casualties in those cities and in Tokyo, probably few lives were saved. Others reject Utilitarian arguments entirely and point out that the bombings were illegal and immoral. Although the disagreements about the atomic bombings continue, most analysts admit that the bombings of German cities and of Tokyo, late in the war, did little or nothing to assist efforts to end the war. The bombing of Dresden in 1945 – producing 60,000 casualties – was unnecessary. Michael Bess concludes his analysis of the campaigns against civilian centers:

> There can be no excuse, in the end, for the practices of large-scale area bombing and firebombing of cities: these were atrocities, pure and simple. They were atrocities because the Anglo-Americans could definitely have won the war without resorting to them. They were atrocities because, starting in 1944, the Anglo-Americans increasingly possessed both the technology and the know-how to conduct a very different kind of aerial warfare.... But they chose instead to "scorch and boil and bake" tens of thousands of non-combatants.... Here – in this sorry fact – lay the single greatest moral failure of the Anglo-American war effort.[10]

We are left with the question: What if the Allies could *not* have won the war without these bombings? Under those circumstances, would the bombing of civilian centers have passed the moral test? *Which moral test?* We also have to consider the problem in context. As we read personal accounts of the fighting in World War II, we can understand why American forces in the Pacific cheered the news that Hiroshima and Nagasaki had been bombed and that their destruction would bring an end to the war. The question – was the bombing immoral? – was beside the point to exhausted and traumatized warriors. Had they been asked, their understandable reaction likely would have been: immoral, so what? We can go home. In the midst of the Battle of the Bulge, soldiers in Europe might have expressed the same opinion about the bombing of Dresden.

I want to spend a bit more time examining the destruction of Dresden. Historians, artists, and journalists are still debating whether the massive firebombing by Anglo-American forces in February 1945 was in any way justifiable. George Packer, in a 2010 article in *The New Yorker*, argues that the bombing of Dresden was part of a well-established Allied pattern:

> The destruction of Dresden was immoral – Churchill himself later expressed qualms – but it was not irrational, or even unusual. It might well have met the standard of a war crime, but from the point of view of the Allies the raid stood out from hundreds of others only because it went so well.[11]

Was the bombing of Dresden more immoral than the bombing of other German civilian centers? Why? Because it had fewer military/industrial sites? It did have some. Because the war already had effectively been won by the Allies? There are those who insist that we only know this now by hindsight. Because it was an exceptionally beautiful city? This perhaps should cause us deep regret, but mothers, babies, kitchens, pets, and family photographs are as precious in ugly cities as in beautiful ones.

Packer is bothered by the fact that Dresdeners seem totally concentrated on restoring the prewar beauty of Dresden while doing their best to forget their own Nazi affiliation and regrettable anti-Semitism. I think he is right to be troubled by this unwillingness to face their own complicity in immoral acts. We Americans should be troubled by the unwillingness of many of our citizens to display the *Enola Gay* together with the story of what happened to thousands of Japanese civilians in Hiroshima. Packer is surely right that citizens should remember the moral wrongs committed by their nation as well as the wrongs committed against them.

But Packer is concerned that observers and analysts may establish a moral equivalence between victims and perpetrators. Dresden, after all, was a city belonging to the perpetrators; in contrast, Coventry and London were cities of victims. I believe it is wrong to interpret *perpetrators* and *victims* this way. Not all German citizens were perpetrators, nor were all British citizens mere victims. The problem of moral equivalence with respect to civilian bombings is not as complicated as the one described by McMahan between soldiers fighting on the side of a just war and those fighting for the unjust side. To prevent avoidable atrocities, we have laws declaring the legal soldiers on both sides as equivalent; both must be treated humanely. On paper, we accept a similar equivalence among civilians; there are laws forbidding deliberate attacks on civilians. We simply do not obey these laws, and this is doubly immoral; that is, it is immoral in both domains of morality. We don't need a law to tell us that babies, young children, and the domestic pets of civilians on both sides are morally equivalent.

### BUILDINGS AND LANDSCAPES

All sorts of buildings are destroyed in war, many deliberately, some accidentally or through carelessness. We should be deeply moved when we see pictures of neighborhoods and whole cities smashed to pieces. The pictorial review of World War II by Ward and Burns provides dramatic photographs not only of dead soldiers but also of dead cities, of ruins.[12] The visual images are striking, but perhaps we need to do more than *look*; we need to *think*. Both Susan Sontag and, before her, Virginia Woolf considered how the visual arts might move people to actively reject war.[13] Surely many, many such images are available to us now, and yet we still accept war as a way to solve our problems. Perhaps we need to spend time with these pictures and ask: What did this area look like before it was bombed to ruins? What did it mean to the people who lived here? What did the people go through as their homes, businesses, places of worship, railway stations, and civic buildings were destroyed? What was life like here before the destruction? What is it like now?

W. G. Sebald has argued that survivors of catastrophic bombing suffer from an almost willful loss of memory. They keep their horror under control by using "such stereotypical phrases as 'a prey to the flames', 'that fateful night', 'all hell was let loose', 'we were staring into the inferno', … and so on and so forth."[14] But how can such events be described? Writing about the air raids on Germany in World War II, Sebald comments:

> The death by fire within a few hours of an entire city, with all its buildings and its trees, its inhabitants, its domestic pets, its fixtures and fittings of every kind, must inevitably have led to overload, to paralysis of the capacity to think and feel in those who succeeded in escaping.[15]

Sebald then gives us page after page describing the destruction of Hamburg in detail. I read and reread those pages, thought and imagined, until I finally broke down in tears. Then I turned to the account by Jorg Friedrich. Hamburg suffered more than 200 bombing raids during the war, but the bombings of July 1943 were the worst by far:

> The 40,000 deaths from the July 1943 Hamburg raids, in addition to those of Dresden, Tokyo, Hiroshima, and Nagasaki, are codes for the extremes of what can be inflicted by the force of arms….[16]

And:

> As if thrown through a revolving door, 4.5 square miles of Hamburg found itself in a room for three hours not where life dies – that always happens – but life is not possible, where it cannot exist. Hamburg and Hiroshima are symbols denoting a war that isolates certain regions from the world of life.[17]

Sebald tells the story of a reporter writing from Hamburg in the fall of 1946:

> That on a train going at normal speed it took him a quarter of an hour to travel through the lunar landscape between Hasselbrook and Landwehr, and in all that vast wilderness, perhaps the most horrifying expanse of ruins in the whole of Europe, he did not see a single living soul.[18]

The carpet bombings of German cities were indefensible from the perspective of just war theory. But so were the German bombings of England. England suffered 23,000 civilian casualties by the end of 1940 and 40,000 by the end of the war. As might be predicted, there were many in England who wanted retaliation, but there were also those who urged restraint. The pacifist Vera Brittain, with five other women, sent an open letter to the prime minister:

> "The Government's own avowed intention of winning the sympathy of the German people would be ruined by this terrible expedient," she wrote.... Even if Germany bombed English cities, England must refuse to retaliate: "It would not help us that German women and children should join us in our agony." ... But, Brittain's letter enraged one woman reader: "There is no reason whatsoever why German women should be spared anything that our own people have previously experienced at the hands of their menfolk." If Germany bombed England, England should BOMB THEM, she capitalized, back.[19]

The second woman saw "no reason whatsoever" for British restraint. The moral reasoning of many adults regressed to that of not very bright fifth graders: "He did it first" and "They did it, too!"

There are many accounts of the destruction of places of worship, gardens, stained-glass windows, artworks, statues, trees, libraries, public buildings, and houses in World War II. In some cases, buildings that had been carefully preserved for several centuries were destroyed. Attempts were made by citizens to save stained-glass paintings by removing the panes and storing them:

> Having been made for the light, they turned milky and disintegrated at the slightest dampness. In all of the Rhineland by the middle of 1942, there was hardly any original glass still in its original fittings.[20]

In the Pacific war, whole villages were wiped out and tiny islands became wastelands:

> The vicious conquest of earth's crust created gaping environmental scars. There was a limit to what even the most potent poisonous agents could accomplish [to exterminate pests]. So American troops threw themselves against nature with muscle and mechanical power, too, hacking and slashing at it.... To create fields of fire, bulldozers uprooted dense undergrowth of brush and scrub. To deny snipers cover, they erased cane fields.[21]

Many civilians were killed, women were raped, and many lost their homes as American forces moved from island to island:

The rows of dead formed … horrifying spectacles. Some 22,000 civilians on Saipan died. An estimated 100,000 civilians lost their lives in the battle for Manila. Figures on Okinawa's civilian casualties range from 80,000 to 160,000, one third of the population.[22]

And the land, too, suffered:

Firepower targeted landscape as much as humans, as blasts blew away vegetation and churned earth to get at the fanatical foe underneath. By the third day of fighting on Betio [in the Solomons], the islet was "bare except for the stumps of trees." … "[N]ot a leaf remained on a tree in what had once been dense jungle."[23]

It is not my purpose here to document the destruction caused by war, nor is it to lay blame on only one side. The destruction has been documented in volume after volume. The point is to ask ourselves why these accounts have not had greater effect. I am revisiting the problem discussed by Woolf and Sontag. Why is it that many of us are deeply moved by visual art, fiction, and firsthand accounts of destruction and yet accept war as a means of resolving conflict or defending ourselves?

The examples I've chosen for this section come mainly from World War II because that war is often referred to as the "good war." After producing volumes of work describing terror and destruction and collecting stacks of photographs depicting piles of bodies and rubble, nations still seek scientific and political solutions to war. When political efforts fail and war ensues, they turn to technology to win the war. Jonathan Glover concludes:

To avoid further disasters, we need political restraints on a world scale. But politics is not the whole story. We have experienced the results of technology in the service of the destructive side of human psychology. Something needs to be done about this fatal combination. The means for expressing cruelty and carrying out mass killing have been fully developed. It is too late to stop technology. It is to the psychology that we should now turn.[24]

### LOSS OF SOCIAL SELF AND MORAL IDENTITY

War destroys bodies, buildings, and the natural environment. In addition, it often causes significant damage to the sense of self and to moral identity. When criminal violence is embedded in war, the losses are grievous. Primo Levi, who spent time as a prisoner in Auschwitz, wrote about the misery suffered by both victims and perpetrators in the Nazi concentration camps:

> We do not wish to abet confusions, small-change Freudianism, morbidities, or indulgences. The oppressor remains what he is, and so does the victim. They are not interchangeable. The former is to be punished and execrated (but, if possible, understood), the latter is to be pitied and helped; but both, faced by the indecency of the irrevocable act, need refuge and protection, and instinctively search for them. Not all, but most – and often for their entire lives.[25]

Levi's comments are extraordinary. He does not excuse the oppressor – he should be punished – but he believes nonetheless that the oppressor needs some kind of refuge. He needs a chance to atone for his guilt and, perhaps, to regain his moral identity. This assumes that at least some of the oppressors were once people who lived by what we have been calling everyday – "commonly accepted" – morality. Those who were never troubled by a moral conscience will probably seek neither refuge nor protection; they will, if they can, simply escape and live on without feeling guilt.

Levi mentions the suffering of Jean Amery, who, as a member of the Belgian resistance, was tortured by the Gestapo and, as a Jew, was then sent to Auschwitz. Amery wrote:

> Anyone who has suffered torture never again will be able to be at ease in the world, the abomination of the annihilation is never extinguished. Faith in humanity, already cracked by the first slap in the face, then demolished by torture, is never acquired again.[26]

Neither Amery nor Levi ever really recovered, and both struggled with the temptation to forget and the impossibility of doing so. On the one hand, forgetting seems to be a betrayal of all those who suffered and died; on the other, not forgetting seems at times to be a betrayal of the living and the future. Veterans of combat and civilian survivors of bombings experience similar tensions. Amery committed suicide in 1978, Levi in 1987.

Levi tells us something about the deterioration of the social self in Auschwitz. Prisoners lived like animals:

We endured filth, promiscuity, and destitution, suffering much less than we would have suffered from such things in normal life, because our moral yardstick had changed.... [We had] stolen ... in the kitchen, the factory, the camp, in short, "from the others," from the opposing side, but it was theft nevertheless. Some (few) had fallen so low as to steal bread from their own companions. We had not only forgotten our country and our culture, but also our family, our past, the future we had imagined for ourselves, because, like animals, we were confined to the present moment.[27]

Suicide, Levi writes, was rare under these conditions but much more common after liberation. Why should this be so? Levi suggests that "suicide is an act of man and not of animal,"[28] and the prisoners were living like animals. After liberation, former captives suffered all sorts of guilt: survivors' guilt, guilt for not fighting harder, for not helping others enough, even for living like an animal. When, after a long lapse, one regains a social self, one can feel guilt – however undeserved – for having relinquished it.

For combat veterans, there is often difficulty in regaining the moral self. The social self may deteriorate, but soldiers know that they are still considered *men* by their own people. If they must live like animals for a time, it is because conditions permit nothing else. It is *not* because fellow citizens think of them as animals, pests to be exterminated. But the return to everyday morality can be very difficult.

Consider the contradictions to which young people are exposed in the military. American soldiers are told that they are fighting for freedom; yet in the military, they must give up most of their freedom and simply obey. They cannot decide when to eat, when or where to sleep, when to get up. In all of their previous life, they were told that it is wrong to kill; now they may march and chant, "Kill, kill, kill!" In school, they heard that "all men are equal"; now they live in a rigid hierarchy, and they are not allowed to forget it. In peacetime, they are scorned or ignored for living like this; in wartime, they are honored for giving up the very things they are said to be fighting for.

There are men who enjoy the killing and destruction of warfare, and I'll consider them in the next chapter. Here we are concerned primarily with those who lose their social or moral identity – men who agonize over what they were forced to do or, in moments of madness, chose to do. J. G. Gray comments in his war diary:

> When I read tonight ... the words of a German soldier's diary, that
> he had lost his "Ich", his personality in the long years of this war,
> I shuddered. He spoke for me.... Formerly I tried to be mild and
> kind, now I interrogate the miserable civilians and take pride in
> sternness and indifferency [sic] to their pleas. Perhaps the worst
> that can be said is that I am becoming a soldier.[29]

Gray devotes a long chapter, "The Ache of Guilt," to the problem faced
by some soldiers – guilt over the killing and destruction in which
they participated.[30] But he worries even more about the *lack* of guilt
felt by many. In his own wartime experience, he vacillated between
feeling guilty and worrying that he had lost the moral sensitivity to
feel guilt.

Apparently many Vietnam veterans suffered similar anxieties.
Some (like the soldier who described killing fishermen and kids) felt
guilt immediately after an act they regretted. Others felt guilt much
later. Jonathan Shay has been listening to Vietnam veterans who may
never recover. One had this to say about what happened to him:

> Why I became like that? It was all evil. All evil. Where before, I
> wasn't. I look back, I look back today, and I'm horrified at what
> I turned into. What I was. What I did. I just look at it like it was
> somebody else. I really do. It was somebody else. Somebody had
> control of me.... I never in a million years thought I would be
> capable of doing that. Never, never, never.[31]

The problem persisted when he returned home:

> I carried this home with me. I lost all my friends, beat up my sister,
> went after my father.... I'd be sitting there calm as could be, and
> this monster would come out of me with a fury that most people
> didn't want to be around.... I brought it back here with me.[32]

Some soldiers in Vietnam escaped the loss of personal moral identity through moral luck; that is, they were lucky enough to be given
jobs or to be sent to areas where the need for morally demanding
decisions did not arise. They did not themselves have to kill. But
some of these soldiers, perhaps many, felt keenly the loss of their
group, even national, moral identity. Shay presents the testimony of

many veterans recounting their feeling of moral betrayal, of "what's right."[33] Sometimes the sense of betrayal was directed at officers and the system that treated enlisted men unfairly: incompetence that caused unnecessary deaths, taking credit and medals for heroic acts done by others, meting out punishment for disagreeing with authority. But there was also a sense that the whole system had betrayed their moral beliefs and coerced them, in turn, to betray their own moral identity.

When soldiers start out in combat thinking that they are serving God and country, it is hard to face the many wartime betrayals of "what is right." Vietnam medics have told that they were forbidden to give serum albumin to "gooks" – military or civilian.[34] Another veteran commented on "the systematic destruction of village hospitals, by mortars, by air, by artillery, believing that if these hospitals were destroyed the Viet Cong could not use them."[35]

Consider how devastating it was for Vietnam veterans to return home to face further betrayals. It was right for American citizens to be ashamed of what our country did in Vietnam; it was wrong to blame individual anonymous soldiers for those wrongs. It has been reported that returning vets were cursed and spat upon. (It has been argued recently that these reports have been greatly exaggerated.) Men struggling to regain the social selves lost in months or years of violence and filth were now treated as criminals, not heroes. It is small wonder that, more than forty years later, so many Vietnam veterans still need psychiatric care. The psychologically wounded, especially those who have lost their moral identity, need loving care and support. Commenting on the change in mental state described by Wilfred Owen in his account of combat in World War I, Lorrie Goldensohn remarks, "War's worst murder is the destruction – dulling, blunting – of our capacity to care."[36] In soldiers, this dulling acts as a protection of sorts; in civilians who have not experienced the violence, it is just hypocrisy and insensitivity.

One possible answer to the problems explored here is to move closer to pacifism, and we'll explore that possibility in a later chapter. But what does it mean to "move closer" to pacifism, and if it is unlikely that our nation will do so, how can we educate young people so that they will at least understand what may happen to them in times of war?

After a searching analysis of war poetry, Goldensohn reminds readers of the worry with which I started this chapter:

> One of the most intractable problems in reading and even writing antiwar texts, however, is that representing the horror of war is not the same thing as committing oneself or others to ceasing its practice. Horror is an amazingly elastic sensation. And what Owen earnestly indicts as the "scorching cautery of battle" becomes the next poet's test of manhood; one soldier's savage accusation becomes the next war's recruiting romance.[37]

In this chapter, we have looked at war's destruction. Perhaps some wars are necessary and destruction is unavoidable. We should consider that possibility, but the culture of masculinity and myths of the warrior help to support war and its centrality in human life. We turn to those topics next.

# 3

## Masculinity and the Warrior

Two apparently opposite evolutionary forces predispose males to warfare: a tendency on the one hand to violence and on the other to behave altruistically toward close kin. The evolutionary tendencies are then aggravated by cultural patterns of socialization that elevate "manliness" and the virtues of the warrior over gentler, more peaceable attributes. Centuries of warrior worship have continued to support aggressive evolutionary tendencies. Indeed, when enlightened thinkers began to praise peace and condemn the violence of war, men like Theodore Roosevelt and Henry Cabot Lodge expressed fear that the "race was becoming 'over-civilized' – too soft … the solution … would come from tapping into more primitive instincts, the kind brought out by sport, especially hunting and most of all by war."[1]

### EVOLUTIONARY LEGACIES

Evolutionary biology has shown persuasively that human beings are genetically closer to chimpanzees than to any other biological group, and observational studies have shown that both humans and chimpanzees exhibit a strong tendency toward violence. Richard Wrangham and Dale Peterson raise important questions on this tendency:

> Most animals are nowhere near as violent as humans, so why did such intensely violent behavior evolve particularly in the human line? Why kill the enemy, rather than simply drive him away? Why rape? Why torture and mutilate? Why do we see these patterns both in ourselves and [in] chimpanzees?[2]

Biologists and anthropologists are uncovering more and more evidence on the connection between gender and violence in both humans and chimpanzees. The widespread violence among humans is largely *male* violence. In the United States, "men are almost eight times as likely as women to commit violent crime."[3] Can the gender difference be accounted for by the difference in size and strength between males and females? Available data on same-sex murders, where there is no gender-based advantage for the killer, yield a negative answer to the question:

> What we find from these statistics, gathered from three dozen human communities around the world, is utterly clear and amazingly consistent. Crime statistics from Australia, Botswana, Brazil, Canada, Denmark, England and Wales, Germany, Iceland, India, Kenya, Mexico, Nigeria, Scotland, Uganda, a dozen locations in the United States, and Zaire, as well as from thirteenth- and fourteenth-century England and nineteenth-century America – from hunter-gatherer communities, tribal societies, and medieval and modern nation-states – all uncover the same fundamental pattern … the probability that a same-sex murder has been committed by a man, not a woman, ranges from 92 percent to 100 percent.[4]

The male tendency to violence is frighteningly real. Wrangham and Peterson note that at present "the remedies for male violence occupy the domain of politics, not biological philosophy," but they also hold out hope that, since the tendency to violence is evolutionary, it can change over time.[5] As I've suggested in the first two chapters, however, the problem may be cultural and psychological more than political, and twenty-first-century culture supports a psychology of violence in its very definition of masculinity.

Before concentrating on the culture, however, we should say something about another evolutionary tendency that seems, at first, to oppose the disposition to violence. There is considerable evidence that a basic form of altruism is inherent in humans and in some non-human animals. It occurs most often between blood kin. Indeed, many scientists use an equation – the altruism equation – developed by William Hamilton to predict and describe altruistic behavior.[6] Even before that equation was formulated, mathematically oriented scientists had developed predictive accounts of altruistic behavior and its connection to bloodlines. In his chapter on the contributions of J. B. S. Haldane, Lee Alan Dugatkin writes:

> Haldane was keen on telling people that he would jump into a river and risk his life to save two brothers, but not one; and that he

would do the same for eight cousins, but not seven. Using himself as an example, the point Haldane was trying to make was that the more closely related two individuals are, the greater the probability that one will sacrifice for the other.[7]

The mathematical point, of course, is that with an appropriate number of blood kin saved, the altruistic agent is preserving his or her own genes.

Haldane's life story has something to contribute to both of the evolutionary tendencies we are discussing. His mathematical work on genetics helps to confirm the biological basis for altruism. His participation in World War I illustrates the male tendency to violence. Dugatkin writes:

> He [Haldane] quickly became an officer in the First Battalion in France, and despite the horrific bloodshed of World War I, J. B. S. enjoyed the experience. Indeed, he seems to have taken pleasure in both attacking and even being attacked by the Germans.... In a latter-day essay, ... Haldane goes as far as to say that "he enjoyed the opportunity of killing people" and regarded this "as a respectable relic of primitive man."[8]

As we look more carefully at these two tendencies – male violence and altruism among blood kin – we see that, far from being in opposition, they work together to support war. Before we look at that collaboration, however, we should say a bit more about altruism. The mathematical work of Hamilton and other scientists provides a Darwinian explanation for altruism, but there is more to it than the unconscious operation of genes. In most species, including humans, females are more likely to behave altruistically. Of course, mothers and offspring are blood kin, but physical proximity also plays a role. The infant begins life as part of his or her mother, and after birth the relation continues to be close, body to body. Families provide an environment in which their members live together and depend on one another for both physical and emotional support. This is a natural dependence, one established by the helplessness of human infants and sustained by mutual affection. The continuous work of caregiving encourages the cultivation of moral sentiments favoring altruism.

Something like this natural interdependence is cultivated in other groups where people must live in close proximity. Military groups work at developing a spirit of comradeship so that soldiers will function as a unit while caring deeply about the welfare of their companions. The men of a military company are not usually cousins or blood kin of any sort, but their training establishes a climate of kinship in which many are willing to sacrifice for their "brothers." We'll say more about this when we discuss the cult of the warrior.

Historically, a social form of kinship was established when people began to settle down in agricultural communities. Surely there was occasional violence before that time among wandering groups and bands; the inclination to male violence preceded the organized violence of war. But agriculture and the development of settled communities provided the setting in which war could flourish. First, the increased production of food in permanent settlements made it possible for greater numbers of people to live in proximity. Second, as the population of insiders grew, it became easier to identify those outside the settlement as Others – people who might threaten the property and well-being of residents.

Commenting on the long-term tendency for states (or nations) to displace tribes and bands, Jared Diamond writes:

> Obviously … part of the reason for states' triumph over simpler entities when the two collide is that states usually enjoy an advantage of weaponry and other technology, and a large numerical advantage in population…. [And] the official religious and patriotic fervor of many states make their troops willing to fight suicidally.[9]

Diamond tells us that religion has functioned to transfer wealth and its distribution to kleptocrats but, in addition, it provides another way to move people toward a wider band of altruism. It gives them a sense of likeness or togetherness that forbids killing within the group but, unfortunately, increases the likelihood that they will work together to kill outside groups branded as enemies. Religion and the state work cooperatively to extend natural, genetic altruism.[10] Thus we see that altruism and violence have an odd relationship. In community-like settings, altruism reduces violence; shrinking in upon itself, it tends to justify and support violence across state or national lines. Nothing would unite the peoples of Earth more quickly and effectively than an attack from outer space. Many cultural practices enforce the commitment to in-group loyalty and outsider enmity, and these practices are especially important in male experience.

## MASCULINITY

The dominance of males coupled with cultural exaltation of masculinity has a long history. History really has been the story of *man*kind. The dominance of males is clear and pervasive in the Bible and biblical commentary. In *Answer to Job*, Carl Jung notes that Yahweh seemed to have lost his fleshlike connection to Sophia, the female representation of wisdom:

> Her place was taken by the covenant with the chosen people who were thus forced into the feminine role. At that time the people consisted of a patriarchal society in which women were only of secondary importance. God's marriage with Israel was therefore an essentially masculine affair, something like the Greek *polis*, which occurred about the same time. The inferiority of women was a settled fact.[11]

For present purposes, we need not be concerned with the accuracy of Jung's interpretations but, rather, with the universality of tone and the observation that a woman, group, or whole nation chosen by a dominant male becomes subservient: a woman to her husband, Israel to Yahweh, the Christian church to Jesus. In a discussion of the last relationship, Jung notes: "Heaven is masculine, but the earth is feminine. Therefore God has his throne in heaven, while Wisdom has hers on the earth."[12] But this does not restore Sophia to a place of honor beside God; instead she *coincides* with the earth and is totally subject to God.

Jack Miles, in a more nuanced, complex interpretation, grants Wisdom a bit more independence, "for Lady Wisdom speaks not just *for* God but also in her own name *about* God and about her relationship with him."[13] Miles concludes, "it would be mistaken to say that Wisdom now feminizes God's character by being absorbed into it. She remains distinct from him by representing, instead, collective humanity, God's image and God's antagonist."[14] Woman, even as Wisdom, becomes a class of beings or a metaphor, whereas God remains a particular, dominant male character.

Feminist theology has tried in a variety of ways to restore Sophia or Wisdom as a real, independent character, but the effort, while interesting, has had little effect on mainstream religion.[15] All of the great monotheisms have mystical branches that seem to recognize feminine wisdom or the presence of God on earth (Shekhina), but again, these subgroups and their poetic thinking have had little political influence on the mainstream institutions and have sometimes been accused of heresy. Early attempts to include forms of feminine wisdom were attacked as vestiges of goddess religion and were overpowered by warnings and myths that associated women with evil, not wisdom.[16] As I have argued elsewhere, the whole program of monotheism is so completely soaked in masculinity that women would do well, even if heartsick, to abandon institutional religion.[17]

Treatment of the feminine and masculine in religious history is a fascinating topic – one that could carry us into volumes of discussion and distraction. The purpose of my brief reference to it here is to underscore the role that religion has played in supporting and elaborating upon the concept of masculinity. As we move into a discussion of the warrior, we'll see that the male biological inclination toward violence has been supplemented, aggravated, and glorified by a near-worship of the masculine warrior.

As Jung noted, the Greek celebration of masculinity and patriarchy in the polis occurred at about the same time as the biblical accounts of Israel's beginnings. Women are not simply regarded as of secondary importance in Greek thought; they are held in contempt. American students today are often taught that democracy, our cherished form of government, began in Athens. Indeed, the text I studied in high school declared that the Athenian government was "completely democratic." More recent texts still laud Athenian democracy but admit that participation in that democracy was denied to slaves, resident aliens, and women. Further, most political offices were held by wealthy upper-class men. Certainly many of the customs and procedures we use today as part of our democratic machinery are a legacy from Athens, but we can hardly recognize life in classical Athens as a democratic way of life. It was a highly classed society, one constantly at war, contemptuous of women, and supportive of slavery.

One might offer Plato's recommendations in Book V of the *Republic* as evidence that not all Athenians insisted on the inferiority of women. In that work, Plato has Socrates argue that intellectually gifted women should be included in the elite group of the republic's guardians. Socrates tries to convince his audience that rationality and intellectual capacity are not limited to the male sex, but he admits that many men will find these ideas "ridiculous." On this, he was clearly right. In a prestigious 1968 translation of the *Republic*, Allan Bloom calls the recommendations for female guardians "absurd conceits." Susan Moller Okin quotes Bloom in her comments:

> Book V, Bloom concludes, "in its contempt for convention and nature, in its wounding of all the dearest sensibilities of masculine pride and shame, the family, and statesmanship and the city" is "preposterous, and Socrates expects it to be ridiculed." Its purpose is, Bloom alleges, to prove to Aristophanes that Socrates can write a funnier comedy than he.[18]

There are, of course, other writers who think Bloom is wrong on this – that Socrates was indeed serious in his comments about female guardians. And it might be that Bloom's comments were directed only at the society in which Socrates and Plato lived. If that is the case, it is unfortunate that he did not make his intention clear.

More important for present purposes is that Plato finds nothing in women *as women* that should be valued. Instead, he makes the daring assertion that women can think and conduct themselves rationally *like men*. Masculinity is given a slight tug away from the male sex, but its essence is not challenged. That tug can be largely countered if we put greater emphasis on biological/emotional factors, and that sort of argument is still popular today. It is still argued, for example, that women, regardless of their intellectual excellence, are "too soft, too emotional" to exercise political or military leadership.

Biblical accounts and Greek philosophy (Aristotle especially) agree on another matter that supports masculinity. Both argue that people should direct their love upward. Yahweh demands that his people love (worship) him. This strikes many mothers as an odd reversal of the way things should be (and, for us, the way things really are). Mothers freely love their children and commit themselves to a continuing love that may or may not be reciprocated; that first "my little darling" is never abandoned. Okin also writes of this odd Greek expectation that the "better" should be loved more than he loves:

> And thus Aristotle concludes that it would be ludicrous for a wife to expect her affection to be returned in a similar way, just as it would be ludicrous for man to expect the same of God; "for it is the part of a ruler to be loved, not to love, or else to love in another way."[19]

In this tradition, love is owed, not felt. Those in power *deserve* love. We have already seen a manifestation of this attitude in Holmes's reversal of thinking on war: a felt hatred while he was in battle and later admiration for young men who thoughtlessly, obediently, gave what they believed they owed. We'll see something like it again and again as we continue to explore what supports war.

Identification of the masculine with that which is "higher," and thus more deserving of love and respect, is thoroughly embedded in most human cultures. I've argued that there are biological roots to male aggression, but there is also a heavy layer – multiple layers – of socialization that maintains it. Religion and philosophy have provided a sturdy foundation for that socialization.

After a discussion of the structural violence associated with patriarchy (the hierarchy and customs established by male dominance), James Gilligan writes:

> If humanity is to evolve beyond the propensity toward violence that now threatens our very survival as a species, then it can only do so by recognizing the extent to which the patriarchal code of honor and shame generates and obligates male violence. If we wish to bring this violence under control, we need to begin by reconstituting what we mean by both masculinity and femininity.[20]

This will be a difficult task given the biological and cultural-historical foundation on which patriarchy has been built. In the previous century, we saw dramatic changes in the status of women, but most of the changes rest on the notion that women, given appropriate opportunities, can be just like men. We have not made much progress in reevaluating the attributes associated (rightly or wrongly) with the sexes, nor have we given enough thought to elevating the work of the caring professions – long the province of women. "Men's work" is still valued more highly, and a woman's status rises when she shows herself capable of doing that work.

Michael Kimmel, in his analysis of male sexual behavior, notes that the rules of masculinity and femininity are strictly enforced and that gender differences are used to maintain the power of men over women. "Manhood is a relentless repudiation and devaluation of the feminine."[21] The problem is complicated, however, because there are elements of the "feminine" as it has been socially constructed that *should be* repudiated by women as well as men. As Virginia Woolf said some years ago, both manliness and womanliness as socially constructed are hateful. Each feeds on the other. Women's acceptance of subordination feeds men's hunger for power; men's blustering strength encourages women to seek protection.

What is needed is a move away from discussion of genderized attributes to a critical and appreciative examination of experience, both male and female but especially female. I would neither accept nor exclude Jungian analysis in this project. Like contemporary feminist Jungians, I reject Jung's essentialist definition of archetypes and his tendency to describe the world in terms of opposites, but I would study new, fascinating interpretations of the archetype concept with the purpose of strengthening theoretical approaches to the analysis of female experience.[22] It is almost certainly more important to study women's experience and its implications for philosophy, religion, and politics than to further analyze male experience. Yet we must make a critical effort. The latter is so heavily colored by the cultural construction of masculinity that it is hard to cut through that construction to see the incredible harm it has caused. When courageous men have attacked the myths of the warrior, for example, other men have embellished those myths to make them even stronger. The attack by Yeats on Owen illustrates this strategy.

## WARRIORS

Several World War I poets contributed greatly to the effort to remove the glory from war and describe its destruction, terror, pain, and filth. Wilfred Owen powerfully denounced "the old Lie: Dulce et decorum est/ Pro patria mori" – a lie dating back to Horace and perennially dusted off and retold. As we noted earlier, the pity and suffering described by Owen outraged the Nobel Prize–winning poet W. B. Yeats, who refused to include Owen's poetry in an anthology he edited. Yeats saw war as a natural and political necessity. In contrast, many of the World War I poets saw it as monumental human folly. The ambivalence over war persisted beyond "Yeats's deploring the unmanly and unimaginative decadence of Wilfred Owen's version of realism, all the way to the guilt-soaked poetry of the Vietnam veteran."[23]

The vacillation between revulsion and delight toward war has appeared in literature since Homer. J. G. Gray, writing of World War II, commented on the attractions of war: "the delight in seeing, the delight in comradeship, the delight in destruction."[24] By the first, he meant "war as a spectacle, as something to see."[25] Seth Schein, in his study of the *Iliad*, points out that "'delight' (charme) is Homer's word for the joy of battle which warriors 'remember' (memnemai) and call on their comrades to 'remember' in the uttermost stress of fighting."[26] The ambivalence toward war is further described:

> The aim of war [the Trojan war] is to destroy a socially evolved human community just like the community that each Greek left behind him when he set sail for Troy. The price of individual self-assertion and self-fulfillment is social annihilation. From the point of view that sees human beings as by definition social, the Greeks, cut off from their homes and families, are in effect less human than the Trojans. From a point of view that sees war as the only way for a human being – or, rather, a human male – to exist meaningfully, the Greeks are more successfully, and therefore more fully, human than the Trojans.[27]

From the second viewpoint, apparently embraced by Yeats and at least reluctantly admired by Holmes, Owen is accused of being unmanly, a person who sees no delight whatever in war. Indeed, the Greek word for courage means "manliness," and the masculine tradition has elevated the warrior's courage to the apex of virtue. Paul Tillich comments:

> Since the greatest test of courage is the readiness to make the greatest sacrifice, the sacrifice of one's life, and since the soldier is required by his profession to be always ready for this sacrifice, the soldier's courage was and somehow remained the outstanding example of courage.[28]

Present-day studies of the *Iliad* tend to emphasize the bloodthirsty, cruel behavior that pervades the poem and to condemn contemporary military activity that resembles it. Simone Weil, for example, sees even the warrior-heroes as victims of "force" or "might" – "that which makes a thing of anybody who comes under its sway."[29] In his comments on Weil's essay, Schein expresses appreciation for much of it but finds it anachronistic in imposing Christian values on the Homeric age. In particular, he says, Weil "fails to recognize the nobility and glory of the slayers along with the humanity and pathos of the slain."[30] Once again, we encounter the ambivalence that pervades the human attitude toward war. Even if Schein is correct that

Weil imposes her Christian values on the *Iliad*, she is surely right in recognizing and deploring the loss of control that combat induces in "noble" warriors.

That loss of control is described in a psychological study of "berserkers" by Jonathan Shay. Achilles, writes Shay, has long been the great hero of warriors, but he "is also the prototype of the berserker."[31] What causes soldiers to enter this frenzied state? For Achilles, the death of Patroclus pushed him into a fury, but it was not only grief that drove him. It was also a sense of shame and guilt because he had not been there to protect his friend. Sometimes men in combat feel this sort of survivor's guilt even though, realistically, they could have done nothing to prevent their comrade's death.

There are many other reports of soldiers becoming exhilarated by battle without quite entering the berserk state. Dexter Filkins reports from Iraq:

> At the base camp of the Fifth Marine Regiment, just outside Diwaniya, two sharpshooters sat on a berm and swapped tales of combat. They'd just climbed off a helicopter, and their eyes were aflame. "We had a great day," Sergeant Eric Schrumpf told me. "We killed a lot of people."[32]

One wonders whether these men, like Shay's berserkers, will take something horrible home that will remain with them forever.

Shame, guilt, fear, and resentment may build up over time in combat, and then a relatively small event – the sight of one's own blood from a slight wound – can send a soldier into a bloodthirsty rage. In a mad rampage, he cannot stop himself and may mutilate the corpse of his enemy, destroy his home, murder his children. Even his comrades may fear to get in his way. Throughout this book, I'm concentrating on *understanding* the features of war and peace and their psychological effects on human beings, but understanding that we may lose our moral control will not necessarily prevent that from happening. When we are engaged in war or have it visited upon us, we are in a different moral (or immoral) world.

Sometimes the berserker state is triggered by hopelessness. A soldier may believe that he is "going to die anyway" and fly into a killing rage until he is killed or falls exhausted. In the berserker state, he is a wild animal, neither a social animal nor human. Shay points out that Homer frequently refers to warriors as beasts, and Achilles' disconnection from the social community is dramatic. On the one hand, he is a beast, separated even from his usual moral behavior as a warrior. On the other hand, he is like a god – nothing can hurt him and everyone around him is aghast with admiration. Beast and god – that awful ambivalence again. At the end of his study of combat trauma, Shay writes:

> On the basis of my work with Vietnam veterans, I conclude that the berserk state is ruinous, leading to the soldier's maiming or death in battle – which is the most frequent outcome – and to life-long psychological and physical injury if he survives. I believe that once a person has entered the berserk state, he or she is changed *forever*.[33]

In our quest for understanding, however, we must attend to stories that challenge the conclusion that the berserk state always produces long-term harmful changes. Daniel Inouye, who served effectively in the U.S. Senate, experienced a berserk episode in World War II. He describes how he destroyed two German machine-gun nests before his right arm was almost blown off by an enemy rifle grenade:

> Then, according to the men and according to my company commander, I went berserk. I had a Thompson submachine gun and with my left hand started approaching the last machine-gun nest, just firing into it with the blood splattering out, and it was a horrible sight. And finally I got hit again on my leg and I kept rolling down the hill, and that was the end.[34]

Perhaps it makes a difference what induces the berserker state. If it is induced by a desperate effort to save one's comrades (as in Inouye's case) and a sense that one is going to die anyway, perhaps success combined with the good motive purges the worst elements of the berserker state.

I mentioned earlier that one of the "delights" of war is a special comradeship. Military training encourages this strong sense of comradeship – "all for one and one for all." It tries – for the most part successfully – to replicate in its soldiers the genetic altruism discussed earlier. On the positive side, a strong sense of comradely loyalty triggers genuine affection and friendship. On the negative side, it may strengthen contempt for the lives of opponents and, of course, the loss of a comrade may be followed by even greater brutality in battle.

Not only do soldiers delight in comradeship, but civilians delight in stories about such comradeship. Filkins gives an account of comradeship among young marines in Iraq:

> They might have been kids, but they were leaner and tougher than their counterparts in Manhattan and Santa Monica.... Sometimes they wrestled over the packets of M&Ms that came in their rations. They sang together the songs they knew.[35]

But:

> There wasn't any point in sentimentalizing the kids; they were trained killers, after all. They could hit a guy at five hundred yards or cut his throat from ear-to-ear.[36]

In warfare, soldiers retain some of the social attributes that are favored in the domain of ordinary morality, but they shift swiftly to the frightening ways of military morality. It's small wonder that character is so often shattered.

The idea of the strong, manly, courageous warrior has persisted. It is perhaps a little less politically correct today to brag about our fighting skills than it was a century ago. But, if we were under attack, audiences might again thrill to hear Theodore Roosevelt's expressed love of war. Evan Thomas writes of Roosevelt's speech encouraging war:

> "All the great masterful races have been fighting races," he barked.... Then he continued: "No triumph of peace is quite so great as the supreme triumphs of war.... Cowardice in a race, as in an individual, is the unpardonable sin." ... By the time Roosevelt concluded his address, he had repeated the word "war" sixty-two times.[37]

William James, living at the same time as the war lovers Roosevelt and Lodge, could not bring himself to worship war. He argued that human beings needed to find a "moral equivalent of war: something heroic that will speak to men as universally as war does."[38] But James recognized that we are talking about two very different moral realms: the realm of ordinary morality and one that seems somehow higher – more powerful, less tied down by customary inhibitions:

> The beauty of war in this respect is that it is so congruous with human nature. Ancestral evolution has made us all potential warriors; so the most insignificant individual, when thrown into an army in the field, is weaned from whatever excess of tenderness

toward his precious person he may bring with him, and may easily develop into a monster of insensibility.[39]

James, of course, is talking about *men* and, although he spoke powerfully against war, he did not object to the manliness that supports it. Indeed, he asked whether war might be man's only "bulwark against effeminacy."[40] Women do not seem to have inherited the evolutionary tendency to be warriors. However, more than an evolutionary tendency is needed to support war. In this chapter, we have looked at the role of masculinity and the glorification of the warrior as factors supporting war. We turn next to another cultural factor that is powerful – patriotism.

# 4

# Patriotism

Jared Diamond has pointed out that both ideology and religion can work toward cementing insider allegiance, an allegiance that can create a society that "becomes much more effective at conquering other societies or resisting attacks."[1] But, of course, the sort of allegiance we call patriotism often promotes hatred, enmity, and enormous sacrifices of life and property. In this chapter, we'll examine the ambiguities of patriotism.

## STARTING WITH CHILDREN

Saluting the flag and reciting the Pledge of Allegiance have long been accepted as the way to start the American school day. Many Americans believe that this custom has been there from the start and, therefore, hold it almost sacred. In fact, the Pledge was written in 1892 to celebrate the unity of a nation of immigrants and to commemorate the opening of the Chicago World's Fair. It was written by Francis Bellamy, a Christian socialist, who "thought it would be a fine thing if on that day all the schoolchildren of America, in unison, offered something to their nation."[2] The now familiar phrase "under God" was added during the presidency of Dwight Eisenhower, and its purpose was mainly to distinguish the United States as a nation of believers in contrast to the Soviet Union and atheistic communism. The Pledge thus acted both to bring people together and to establish an important difference.

There are jokes about small schoolchildren reciting the Pledge and badly mispronouncing words they cannot understand. One solution to this problem would be to introduce the Pledge at a later time, after students have some understanding of the words; another would be to abandon the practice entirely. A third would be to continue the practice as an early ritual of solidarity but follow it in the middle school years with a study of the history, meaning, and confusion that have grown up around it. However, American history textbooks rarely discuss the origins of and arguments over familiar rituals. Acknowledging ambiguities is the first step in accepting, rejecting, or resolving them, but some citizen-critics object to the inclusion of any material in school textbooks that challenges the master narrative, a story of heroic and God-blessed nation-building. Part of that narrative is stated by Cynthia Dunbar, a Christian fundamentalist and member of the Texas school board:

> We as a nation were intended by God to be a light set on a hill to serve as a beacon of hope and Christian charity to a lost and dying world.[3]

Many of us today would like to find a way to move toward a more universal sense of citizenship, to shape our patriotism toward an acceptance of global needs and contributions, and we'll discuss the possibility of developing a cosmopolitan form of patriotism. However, given views such as Dunbar's, it is hard to see how more than the most innocuous attempts at cosmopolitanism or world citizenship can be included in public school textbooks. Indeed, the very idea of non-partisan objectivity is sometimes condemned. When attempts along these lines were made in the 1930s, an official of the Daughters of Colonial Wars attacked books that "tried to give the child an unbiased viewpoint instead of teaching him real Americanism."[4]

As part of their introduction to patriotism, young children are subjected to learning the words of "The Star-Spangled Banner" and trying to sing it. Again, many people believe that it has been our national anthem since the time it was written during the War of 1812, but it was not designated the national anthem until 1931. As a fiery symbol of patriotism, it tends to support war, rallying citizens to fight for liberty and justice. Many citizens would prefer to adopt "America the Beautiful" as our national anthem – it is easier to sing! – but it could hardly be used to support war; it pledges us to exercise self-control and to extend brotherhood from "sea to shining sea."

Patriotism is instilled in children by songs, poetry, and stories of military heroes. Outside of school, some holidays increase patriotism and support war. Independence Day, July 4, is a much-loved celebration of the nation's birth. Flags fly, bands play martial music, people march in parades, men reenact famous battles, cannons are fired, and marvelous displays of fireworks complete the day. Families and neighbors get together and enjoy hot dogs, potato salad, ice cream, popsicles, corn, and all sorts of drinks. It is a wonderful day that many of us love. But, without wrecking the fun, we should remind one another that it is still a ritual that celebrates and supports war.

Sports too play a role in supporting war. Many competitive games take on the appearance of battles, and audiences increase the excitement and partisanship with shouts and chants. Martha Nussbaum (whose ideas on cosmopolitanism we will discuss shortly) comments on the use of the chant "U-S-A, U-S-A" as an example of fans' assertive support for both team and country:

> This chant seemed to express a wish for America to defeat, abase, humiliate its enemies. Indeed, it soon became a general way of expressing the desire to crush enemies, whoever they are. [It was used when the umpire made a bad call against the home team.] ... It's not surprising that Stoic philosopher and Roman emperor Marcus Aurelius, trying to educate himself to have an equal respect for all human beings, reports that his first lesson was "not to be a fan of the Greens or Blues at the races, or the light-armed or heavy-armed gladiators at the circus.[5]

Some may feel that Nussbaum exaggerates the role of competitive games in encouraging "us–them" thinking – after all, "it's just fun" – but I think her point is a good one. I remember that I, as a high school student, skipped out on pep rallies because the rhythmic and mindless chanting reminded me of the shouting Nazi crowds we then saw on newsreels. I didn't fully understand my own reaction at the time, but I know that I felt a genuine revulsion. Schools should encourage teenagers to think about such activities and the emotional reactions they induce. What is operating here besides "just fun"?

Schoolchildren are indoctrinated with the Pledge, patriotic poetry and songs, national holidays, and carefully worded historical accounts. Most of them are enthusiastic national citizens by the time they enter high school, and many adult citizens would argue that this is a good thing.

Education for patriotism displays contradictions similar to those we've seen in attitudes toward war. A curriculum guide written in 1909 starts with a surprising whole-world view, describing love of country in Asiatic islands, Ethiopia, Malta, and Norway.[6] But in its third point, it takes a highly nationalistic view:

> There has probably never been a country for which so much hardship and suffering have been endured in bringing about the present condition of liberty, culture, and personal welfare. Think of the thousands who have toiled, suffered, and died for it! We have a country we can love, because there have been *patriots* who loved their country better than they loved themselves. No nation has had such splendid heroes, and they are more in number than we can name.[7]

The examples included in the set of lessons on patriotism are almost entirely national and connected to the military. However, this emphasis is interrupted once more in item 11:

> There is, of course, something higher than patriotism, and that is the *love of humanity* at large. We should never allow our love for our own countrymen to shut out the larger love of our fellow men. The world is larger than any country in it.[8]

But this insight is not elaborated upon, and the overwhelming impression is one of nationalistic fervor, loyalty, and sacrifice: "Let him in his heart hold aloft the flag of our country, and *salute it daily*, as the emblem of the world's hope and inspiration."[9] Here we can anticipate another problem. When love for all of humanity is accompanied by nationalistic patriotism, we might predict a surge of democratic evangelism and, of course, in the last 100 years or so, the United States has often engaged in campaigns to convert the world to democracy.

#### COSMOPOLITANISM AND PATRIOTISM

Martha Nussbaum argues that the ideals often associated with patriotism – justice and equality – would be better served by another ideal, "namely the very old ideal of the cosmopolitan, the person whose allegiance is to the worldwide community of human beings."[10] As we consider this possibility, we should ask what might be gained and what might be lost if we emphasized cosmopolitanism over patriotism in our schools.

In American history, probably the best-known exemplar of cosmopolitanism is Thomas Paine. Schoolchildren usually learn something about Paine's *Common Sense*, a pamphlet that aroused and united early Americans in their opposition to English rule. He was, it seems, an extraordinary patriot. But students rarely hear what he wrote in *The Age of Reason*, where he declared himself a citizen of the world and expressed his commitment to "doing justice, loving mercy, and endeavoring to make our fellow creatures happy."[11] It is remarkable that his writings were instrumental in both encouraging revolution and inspiring generations of nonviolent thinkers.

Paine's *Common Sense* was widely admired, but his ideas on nonviolence and cosmopolitanism were often condemned. Years later, Theodore Roosevelt described him as a "filthy little atheist," and Paine's biographer said of him: "Men will learn to express all that is base, malignant, treacherous, unnatural, and blasphemous by one single monosyllable – Paine."[12] Even today, the attitude called *cosmopolitanism* is often equated with anti-Americanism and antipatriotism.

Nussbaum uses Rabindranath Tagore's novel *The Home and the World* to argue for the morally superior attitude of cosmopolitanism. With Tagore, she believes that "nationalism and ethnocentric particularism are not alien to one another, but akin."[13] Thus:

> Once someone has said, I am an Indian first, a citizen of the world second, once he or she has made the morally questionable move of self-definition by a morally irrelevant characteristic, then what, indeed, will stop that person from saying, as Tagore's characters so quickly learn to say, I am a Hindu first, an Indian second, or I am an upper-class landlord first, and a Hindu second?[14]

This paragraph raises an important question for a careful reader: Is national identity a "morally irrelevant characteristic"? Kantian rationalists would certainly support Nussbaum in her claim that basic moral principles transcend national, tribal, and religious affiliations, but others would argue that the interpretations of moral precepts – if not the precepts themselves – differ significantly. National and religious identity may *not* be irrelevant. Certainly Christian fundamentalists in the United States today do not believe this. For them, being an American is a highly relevant moral characteristic.

Further, if people really believe or even half-believe that their own way is morally best, that belief may override the more loosely held cosmopolitan commitment in emergency situations. A person who generally holds a cosmopolitan attitude may become ultrapatriotic in times of war. Indeed, if he adheres to his cosmopolitanism at such times, he may be thought traitorous. In most cases, nationalistic patriotism will win. Consider the example of James Conant, a highly competent and much-admired president of Harvard University. During World War II, he headed both Harvard and a branch of the National Defense Research Committee that was working on chemical, biological, and incendiary weapons, many of which are condemned by both international law and ordinary morality. In a meeting with the Senate Foreign Relations Committee, Conant defended his work on weapons, saying:

> We must bravely do the things that we know ought to be done. And we must lay the moral, intellectual and spiritual foundations for the kind of world we want our children to inherit.[15]

The awful contradictions in Conant's statement (and in his behavior) give weight to Nussbaum's arguments for cosmopolitanism. Surely, one committed to justice and equality for all of humanity could not consider using chemical and biological weapons to destroy opposing nations. Here we see a great weakness in cosmopolitanism – its "thinness," as described by Benjamin Barber. The idea just does not grab us or give us something to cling to passionately. Barber points out that we do not actually live in the whole world described by Nussbaum: "Rather, we live in this particular neighborhood of the world, that block, this valley, that seashore, this family. Our attachments start parochially and only then grow outward."[16]

But Barber makes a mistake when he identifies cosmopolitanism with what others of us would call *exceptionalism*. Barber says, "America's civic nativism is ... a celebration of internationalism, a devotion to values with cosmopolitan reach," and then goes on to claim that

> [t]he cosmopolitanism of such values has even gotten America in trouble (in Mexico under Wilson, in Vietnam under Kennedy, Johnson, and Nixon, and perhaps now in Bosnia) – a reminder to Nussbaum that cosmopolitanism too has its pathologies....[17]

Many of us would, however, label our imperialistic tendencies as examples of exceptionalism, not cosmopolitanism. Supposing that we are custodians of universal values, we eagerly try to impose them on others.

Even as our attachments or concerns grow outward, they tend to encounter limits. Our obligations to those close to us may overwhelm our desire to help those at a distance, and a feeling of personal helplessness may sweep over us as we become aware of the magnitude of the problems facing those at a distance.[18] That said, there should be something sure and solid in our commitment to humanity as a whole that would prevent the utter breakdown we see so pervasively in war.

In war or in the times leading to war, the inclination toward cosmopolitanism gives way to national patriotism. That pressure in itself makes it difficult for anyone to maintain a public attitude of concern for all of humanity or, as often happens (as in Conant's case), a "cosmopolitan" may claim that war and destruction must be pursued in order to spread "true" morality over the whole world. When Jeannette Rankin, in the House of Representatives, opposed the declaration of war against Germany in 1917, she was loudly criticized as "a dupe of the Kaiser, a member of the Hun army in the United States, and a crying schoolgirl."[19] And, of course, she was not reelected for many years. (She was eventually reelected – in time to cast the only vote against declaring war on Japan in 1941; that vote ended her political career.)

Nussbaum acknowledges that "becoming a citizen of the world is often a lonely business."[20] Part of the loneliness lies in the separation from the local and national loyalties that give life special interest and sometimes excitement. The question is whether we can retain some of the color and vibrancy of patriotism and give up the evils associated with it. As Barber puts it, "The question is not how to do without patriotism and nationalism but how to render them safe."[21]

## A CHASTENED PATRIOTISM

Jean Bethke Elshtain suggests a move to *chastened* patriotism, a patriotism that avoids dangerous excesses. She would not reject patriotism:

> Patriotism ... is part of our repertoire of civic ideals and identities. While its excesses may be lamented, it cannot, and should not, be excised, for patriotism also taps love of country that yields civic concern *for* country. Attached more to the sense of a political and moral community than to a state, patriotism can be, and has been, evoked to bring out the best in us – even as, when it shades into nationalism, it can arouse the worst.[22]

What would this patriotism look like?

> But it is a *chastened* patriot I have in mind, men and women who
> have learned from the past. Rejecting counsels of cynicism, they
> modulate the rhetoric of high patriotic purpose by keeping alive
> the distancing voice of ironic remembrance and recognition of the
> way patriotism can shade into the excesses of nationalism....[23]

The spirit of this chastened patriotism seems right, but we need to
explore details of how to produce it. What does it mean to learn from
the past? Even historians do not agree on descriptions of the past,
much less on the lessons to be learned from it. And, if we can agree on
the lessons, how should we pass them along to the young? How do we
deal with those who object to any modulation of patriotic rhetoric?
Where is the line between patriotism and nationalism?

David Tyack notes that "history textbooks, as a whole, had a
strong master narrative in the nineteenth century: Its motif was that
the United States was a favored nation."[24] The narrative is still there,
but its language has changed over time. Today, the textbooks do not
demean African Americans or other minority groups. Immigrant history is celebrated in textbooks, although illegal immigrants are still
criticized and resented in public. Women have been accorded the full
rights of citizenship, and textbooks make an obvious effort to include
the contributions of women. Sometimes the efforts are ludicrous,
because the master narrative is still there, lying beneath current language, and it is only when women have contributed to the continuing
story of the white male political project that they are included. Their
contributions *as women* are rarely recognized, and women's experience is given little attention.[25]

Dramatic changes in the master narrative are resisted even today,
and textbooks try not to offend vociferous groups on the left and right.
Sometimes the curriculum battles are fierce and uncompromising, as
in the debates over evolution and creationism. More often, compro-
mises are made in order to maintain a curriculum and sell textbooks.
There would be a clamor, for example, if Thomas Paine and *Common
Sense* were left out, but textbook writers can, and do, leave out any discussion of his claim to world citizenship and his rejection of theism.
Textbooks usually include Patrick Henry, but they separate his fiery
speeches for independence from his opposition to the Constitution.
Both may be mentioned but separately, often pages apart, as though

they might be the views of two different people. Thus textbooks avoid controversy, but they also sacrifice the real interest such controversy might engender. Indeed, one wonders how young people are to learn anything about "ironic remembrance" if they hear nothing of the passionate disagreements among patriots.

Many of us would like to see American history and social studies organized around issues instead of a bland, chronological presentation of "facts." But if that were done, much more attention would have to be given to, for example, religion, and most current textbooks say little on the subject. They do not even try to correct the commonly held untruth that our nation was founded on Christian principles, despite the fact that George Washington himself said that it was not. This is not to say that our constitutional principles are antithetical to Christianity, nor is it to deny the fact that the nation has always been dominantly Christian. Similarly, there is rarely mention of the fact that many of the Founding Fathers were deists, and the popular textbook on my work table does not even list *secularism* or *deism* in its index. (Nor, for that matter, is there an entry for *peace*.) I'll say more on this in the chapter on religion.

Reformers have tried to introduce issue-oriented curricula, and occasionally they have been successful, but their success has been short-lived. Harold Rugg, a prominent reconstructionist, produced a series of issue-oriented textbooks that sold over a million copies between 1929 and 1939.[26] The textbooks included issues of racism and sexism, wealth and poverty, capitalism and labor, and immigration; they were enormously popular during a time of great economic suffering. By 1940, however, opposition to social reconstruction and Rugg's books became vigorous. He was accused of anti-Americanism, treason, and the promotion of socialism. It may not surprise readers to hear that the opposition was led by the National Association of Manufacturers and the American Legion. It has always been hard to separate patriotism from what is seen as the nation's economic interests.

## UNDERSTANDING PATRIOTISM AND COSMOPOLITANISM

Humanity has made some progress in moving beyond national and cultural parochialism. Most schoolchildren today are exposed to some study of the arts and customs of other cultures, and the denigration of other races is widely rejected. In the United States, although we still have difficulties to overcome, the sort of scornful talk once accepted about African Americans is rightly condemned. This may seem a small accomplishment, but when one considers the language and treatment our black citizens once (not long ago) suffered, it is significant. Still, much of the material offered in multicultural education is bland, devoted to uncontroversial topics such as festivals and various ethnic celebrations. We have acknowledged our shameful history of slavery, lynching, and publicly accepted discrimination against our nation's black citizens, but we still have a difficult time admitting the offenses we have committed against others – Chinese immigrants during the gold rush, Native Americans from coast to coast, Japanese, Korean, and Vietnamese during wartime.

The international response to natural disasters is another commendable sign of growing global understanding – or, at least, global compassion. There is an outpouring of international sympathy and aid when any area of the world is struck by an earthquake, a flood, or a devastating fire. On the other hand, widespread hunger and disease may be quietly ignored for decades. Although the generous international response to disasters is praiseworthy, there is also a less virtuous aspect to it – an almost competitive drive to show who has done the most to relieve suffering. Great disasters provide dramatic opportunities to show how good we are. This suggests again that we need to educate more broadly and deeply for an understanding of patriotism and world citizenship.

When we look with justifiable pride at our generous responses to those suffering a natural disaster, we might also pause to reflect on how it happens that our sympathy can be so easily changed to hatred. How is it that we will predictably reach out to help a given people at one time and, when our country labels the same people enemies, we will reluctantly or enthusiastically kill millions of them?

I want to consider four areas to which we should give more attention in an attempt to reconcile patriotism and cosmopolitanism: concern for our standing in the world, pride in our heritage, pride in the principles for which our country stands, and love of place. These centers of interest represent both opportunities and roadblocks.

Americans are particularly and peculiarly afflicted with a concern for our standing in the world. As the world's only superpower at the start of the twenty-first century, the temptation to retain and extend the reputation for being *first* or *best* is both understandable and deplorable. Succumbing to the fervor that accompanies being number one leads to strutting and bragging in the name of patriotism. It leads also to the corruption of truth. On the one hand, we are number one in military expenditures, spending at least as much as or more than the rest of the world combined on our military. On the other hand, we are also number one in the percentage of our population imprisoned, but we cannot brag about this. During the current (2010) debate over health care, many of our politicians claimed that America has the best health care in the world, although this contention is easily refuted by looking at the statistics on maternal and infant mortality, life expectancy, the extent of childhood malnourishment, and the occurrence of asthma and obesity. In other areas, there seems to be a blind acceptance of the idea that being number one is in itself a significant goal. For example, President Barak Obama recently warned that other nations are now producing a greater proportion of college graduates than America, and he urged that we work to reclaim our position as first in this project. Why? Do we really need more college graduates? In America, there is little need to answer this question. Being number one is still thought to be a praiseworthy goal in itself.

There is, however, another sense of standing in the world that should concern all citizens. We should be concerned with our reputation as good citizens in the global community of nations. It is hard for public schools to include accounts of acts for which our nation might be accused of wrongdoing. These matters are often given open-minded attention at our best colleges and universities, but many citizens are left out of this discussion, and they are not formally introduced to issues that require national self-reflection. Generous, self-critical thinking should be promoted in schools as soon as children are capable of such thinking, but it is strongly resisted by groups who want children to hear a consistent story of American goodness.[27] Pushing for a change in the school curriculum that would describe the United States as a Christian nation, one advocate said, "The philosophy of the classroom in one generation will be the philosophy of government in the next."[28] Many people opposed to teaching children anything critical about their country take the issue very seriously.

Readers should pause for a few minutes here and ask themselves why it is so hard for many people to see our history as an enormously complicated, morally uneven story. We want our children, as individuals, to admit when they are wrong and make amends to those they have harmed, and yet a similar attitude to national behavior is often regarded as unpatriotic. It does make sense to handle these matters in age-appropriate ways and to balance the good and bad so that students can think critically without becoming cynical.

Pride in our heritage certainly should have a place in educating for patriotism, but pride, like criticism, should be encouraged in an open-minded and critical way. Barbara Tuchman has written about the intellectual talent and character of America's Founders. Her approach is exemplary:

> For all their flaws and quarrels, the Founding Fathers have rightfully been called by Arthur M. Schlesinger, Sr., "the most remarkable generation of public men in the history of the United States or perhaps of any other nation." It is worth noting the qualities this historian ascribes to them: they were fearless, high-principled, deeply versed in ancient and modern political thought, astute and pragmatic, unafraid of experiment....

And she continues with a matter she regards as significant:

> [They] were "convinced of man's power to improve his condition through the use of intelligence." That was the mark of the Age of Reason that formed them, and although the 18th century had a tendency to regard men as more rational than in fact they were, it evoked the best in government from these men.[29]

Think what might be done by a thoughtful teacher with this passage. It would supplement the learning of facts about the Articles of Confederation, the Constitutional Convention, and biographical information on the participants. It would draw students' attention to Tuchman's use of another historian's evaluation. The glowing approbation is not presented as a fact but as a considered, well-founded interpretation. And to what is Tuchman alluding when she writes "for all their flaws and quarrels"? Perhaps students will read Charles Beard's *An Economic Interpretation of the Constitution of the United States* or other works that discuss the personal and regional concerns of the Founders.

The discussion can be brought right up to current debates. Tuchman attributes the attitudes of the Founders to their immersion in the Age of Reason, whereas some present-day critics insist that the Founders were primarily influenced by their Christianity. Discussion of issues concerning the Founders and their purposes should be aimed at a search for evidence and at an increased willingness to listen to well-considered arguments – not so much at firm conclusions. Conducting discussions of this kind is difficult in any social setting, but it is especially difficult in schools. Too many teachers want their students to arrive at the "right answer," and there are political groups that also take this position, insisting that inclusion of the "other side" involves indoctrination or, worse, the promulgation of falsehoods. Because it is so contentious to treat unsettled conflicts, most schools either omit them entirely or wait for an authoritative consensus that enables them to teach once-controversial ideas as facts.

Perhaps a good way to start is with a semicontroversial issue that has been largely (but not totally) resolved. The theory of evolution is a case in point. Scientific evidence strongly supports evolution, and most schools include it among the facts of biology, although arguments for creation science and intelligent design are pressed in various parts of the country. Typically, when a state or local school board has decided that it is true, evolution becomes part of the curriculum. I will not argue that intelligent design should be taught as an alternative, because the evidence for evolution is conclusive. However, I do think students should hear about the history of the debate. It is too exciting to ignore, and discussing it gives students an opportunity to think about how controversial issues might be handled. Students should hear not only of Darwin but also of T. H. Huxley, Bishop Wilberforce, Jean-Baptiste Lamarck, William Paley, Alfred Russel Wallace, and current thinkers on the topic. Some argue that material on the history and debates over evolution does not belong in science class; instead, it should be included in a history of science course – a course that almost never appears in the secondary school curriculum. Thus the controversy is handily dismissed. If our object is to teach students something about rationality and reasoning, then we simply must discuss such matters broadly and sensitively where and when they arise. The narrow compartmentalization of subject matter in our schools works against the development of reason and intellect.

I've used the topic of evolution as an example of a conflict that does culminate in a scientifically approved right answer and, in teaching about the conflict, teachers should inform students of the scientific consensus. But there are other matters on which students might be invited to collect and assess the evidence. What role did Christianity play in the founding of America? Many of us believe that Tuchman was right in pointing out that the Founders lived in the Age of Reason and fashioned the Constitution according to ideas developed without direct reference to Christianity, but this is not to say that Christianity did not influence the thinking of individual Founders. A rightful pride in our American heritage need not depend on stubborn assertion either that the Constitution was based on Christian principles or that Christianity had nothing to do with it.

Unquestionably, several prominent Founders were deists – even some who attended Christian churches; they did not believe, as Christians do, in a personal God. Washington, Adams, and Franklin probably fall into this category. Jefferson and Madison were clearly secularists, not Christian believers. Why does this trouble so many Christians today? The State Board of Education in Texas has recently considered omitting mention of Thomas Jefferson in the school curriculum because he advocated a "wall of separation" between church and state, and at last review they did decide to omit Madison. As noted earlier, there is seldom any recognition of Thomas Paine's purported atheism, and documented differences on matters of religion are generally ignored.

Important questions to be considered in public high schools include the following: Why does it matter so much to some people that the country's Founders be described as Christians? Why do these people insist that the Constitution was based on Christian principles? If it is simply a matter of establishing and teaching the truth, then advocates of the Christian foundation are demonstrably wrong. But this response is almost impossible to make in schools, and it would very likely inflame passions further. If we believe that one important task of education is to promote rationality, then we should point out that, although the Founders thought it best to omit overtly religious principles from their debates about the Constitution, this does not mean that individual members of the Constitutional Convention were not influenced by their own Christian beliefs and backgrounds. Nor does it mean that the principles espoused in the Constitution are anti-Christian. It means only that thoughtful men considered it best to leave references to religious commitments and precepts out of their deliberations. In the interests of rationality and civility, religious commitments were consigned to private life. The success of the Founders in surmounting religious interests is an achievement of which to be proud. Discussed rationally and generously, the topic of America's founding should set an example for contemporary political debate and a continuing commitment to the civil use of reason.

Issues such as these are regularly discussed in our best colleges and universities. Their omission at the secondary school level serves to separate our citizens into two different intellectual groups and to aggravate a growing form of class division. Our public schools are doing an admirable job of teaching children religious tolerance, but they do little to include unbelievers in that tolerance. Probably most high school students could not define (even loosely) *deist, secularist,* or *agnostic*. In the public mind, these terms are somehow associated with positions that are antireligious, anti-Christian, or anti-American. An appreciative study of the deistic leanings of Washington, Adams, and Franklin, together with the secular positions of Jefferson and Madison, should induce defensible patriotic pride. How would such men fare in today's politics?

In a similar vein, careful study of documents such as the Declaration of Independence, the Constitution, and Lincoln's second inaugural address should promote patriotic pride in the principles we have espoused. When honest historical accounts remind us that our record as a nation is not unblemished, we need not descend into angry and cynical condemnation. We can, instead, compare what we have done with our most cherished principles. Educators eager to set the record straight and avoid the saccharine extremes of past teaching sometimes forget that there are things to be proud of, and the young need to believe that there are principles to which they should be committed. Recognizing both failures and brilliant statements of principle is part of an education for rationality and a chastened patriotism.

Can love of place contribute to a healthy patriotism? Patriots are often willing to fight and die for the particular place they identify as their country. A patriotic love of place seems to be universal; the loved place is associated with a sense of ownership – this is *my* (our) place, and I must protect it from invaders and outsiders who would take it from me or warp its nature. The love of place is so strong that national leaders sometimes use it as an excuse to wage war – "protect our land" – when there is no actual threat to their homeland.

The actual loss of the homeland is a real tragedy. When we read of the longing for home expressed by displaced people, we are deeply moved. Katherine Platt, writing of the Palestinian displacement, has described how the longing of first-generation persons becomes politicized:

> The literal places of origin so copiously mourned by the older generation became generalized and symbolic. Peasant class position and consciousness was replaced by working class position and consciousness. Clan and village solidarity gradually crumbled and has slowly been replaced by a Palestinian national identity.[30]

But this identity longs to be rooted in actual places, although those expressing it may have little recollection of those places. The first generation longed for particular neighborhoods, orchards, houses, roads, and landmarks. Later generations are doubly deprived. Not only are they separated from actual places, they are also separated from the memories associated with those places. One cannot brush aside these desperate longings by responding that the Jews have suffered displacement again and again for centuries. Of course, they have, and both tragedies must be recognized. Centuries of Jewish persecution and displacement should be studied and discussed. Feeling the pain of one group does not necessitate hardening one's heart to the other.

Politically, then, love of place seems to be a source of conflict and, when the place is identified with ownership, it continues to be a primary focus for patriotically inspired battle. But there is some reason for hope in the current widespread concern for the welfare of Earth itself. If we love a particular place, we know that its welfare is intimately connected to the health of the Earth on which it exists. This understanding may increase our commitment to a chastened patriotism. Because I love *this* place, I want a healthy Earth to sustain it. If scientists are wrong about climate change and if, in particular, they might be wrong about the effects of human behavior on that change, I should still be willing to take precautionary measures. Thinking this way might be called *ecological cosmopolitanism*, and it is one bright spot in a world crowded with parochial interests. If the well-being of my loved place depends on the well-being of Earth, I have a good reason for supporting the well-being of *your* loved place. I have selfish as well as cosmopolitan reasons for preserving the home-places of all human beings. Cosmopolitanism becomes thicker and more potent with this realization.

In this chapter, we have discussed the pervasive nature of national patriotism – the early indoctrination of patriotism in children and the continuing controversies over the origins of our national government. I have used the United States as the locus of the discussion, but readers from other parts of the world can surely find similar problems and arguments. We have considered the possibility of a chastened patriotism and have found the possibility riddled with difficulties. One of the greatest difficulties is the apparent ease with which national governments can arouse in their populations hatred for the enemies they identify. We turn to that topic next.

# 5

# Hatred

How is it that a population of ordinary, friendly people can be pushed to hatred of other ordinary, friendly people by their leaders? In this chapter, we'll explore the induction and maintenance of hatred during wartime. But war is not the only source of hatred, and we'll have to consider long-standing hatreds that erupt in occasional violence. Already we see a dramatic difference in the possible causal relation. In one case, the violence of war induces hatred; in the other, pre-existing hatred induces warlike violence. Further, attempts at solidifying peace after bitter conflict sometimes trigger new violence in, for example, "solutions" that use ethnic cleansing and mass deportations. Not all periods of "peace" are nonviolent. Finally, hatred induced by past injuries – perceived or real – often supports the acts of extreme violence we call terrorism.

## WAR AND HATRED

Hatred and patriotism often seem to go together:

> Freda Kirchwey, the editor of *The Nation*, wrote a post–Pearl Harbor column: "The fruits of appeasement have burst," she said. "The horror has made America one. Today we love each other and our country. We feel a happy sense of union swelling in our hearts; hatred and contempt for our enemy runs warmly in our blood.[1]

How does this happen? Both patriotic schooling and propaganda play a role; indeed, they build on each other. Before Pearl Harbor, the attitude of Americans toward Japan was one of almost comic scorn for its shoddy products, not one of hatred. But propaganda depicted

Japanese soldiers as physically and psychologically repulsive and fanatical. They became "Japs" and "Nips," and songs included references to the "dirty little Jap." There was little sympathy for the loyal Japanese–American citizens who were interned during the war. For those of us today who have developed both respect and affection for Japanese colleagues and students, these wartime attitudes are hard to recall without embarrassment and shame.

Propaganda encourages hatred and glorifies the sacrifice of patriots. Often civilians are more enthusiastic than military men about war. Robert Graves described the phenomenon in World War I:

> England looked strange to us returned soldiers [on leave]. We could not understand the war-madness that ran wild everywhere, looking for a pseudo-military outlet. The civilians talked a foreign language; and it was newspaper language.[2]

Graves followed this with the text of a letter that appeared in *The Morning Post* and was widely circulated. The letter, "A Mother's Answer to 'A Common Soldier'" by "A Little Mother," urges women to be proud to lose their sons in battle and to maintain a temperature for war at "white heat." It was received as an eloquent statement of loyalty, pride, and courage. Today it reads as a mawkish tribute to the foolishness and horrors of war. Year after year, war after war, mothers (and fathers) have been urged to believe that their sons have not died in vain.

Sometimes, at the beginning of war, there is so little animosity between the opposing forces that generals fear their men will not fight. Before the outbreak of actual hostilities in World War I, German and English soldiers played volleyball together, and it was hard to imagine the awful slaughter to come. But duty to country and loyalty to military commands can both operate effectively to goad men to violence in the absence of hatred. Andrew Fiala quotes Hegel on this:

> "Modern wars are accordingly waged in a humane manner, and persons do not confront each other in hatred." Hegel continues: "At most, personal enmities will arise at military outposts, but in the army as such, hostility is something indeterminate which takes second place to the duty which each respects in the other."[3]

Waged in a humane manner? What philosophical nonsense! We hear a far different story from veterans of actual combat. Theodore

Roosevelt had urged all of his sons to be "manly" and go to war. All four did in World War I:

> Archie recalled the sensation of shooting a German and then, in a rage, stomping on his face, staining his boot with blood up to the ankle. He felt, he later wrote, like a creature "of the Stone Age."[4]

Soldiers, according to Hegel, are supposed to put aside their individual anger and hatred; they should act out of duty. (This is, of course, one aim of just war theory.) Robert Graves points out that, at the start of World War I, the British War Office had taken roughly this position. But that changed:

> Troops learned instead that they must HATE the Germans, and KILL as many as possible. In bayonet-practice, the men had to make horrible grimaces and utter blood-curdling yells as they charged. The instructors' faces were set in a permanent ghastly grin. "Hurt him, now! In the belly! Tear his guts out!" they would scream, as the men charged the dummies. "Now that upper swing at his privates with the butt. Ruin his chances for life! No more little Fritzes!"[5]

Graves comments that he was glad to get away from both civilians and trainers and back to the trenches, where attitudes were less bloodthirsty. Soldiers, in contrast to civilians and trainers, were often sickened by the misery and death of combat. Occasionally, the recognition of common humanity and sheer disgust with destruction overcame all desire to kill the enemy. Sebastian Faulks includes in his World War I novel, *Birdsong*, a moving episode in which a British officer, trapped in a German tunnel, encounters a German officer who is trying to rescue some of his own men. The German lieutenant, Levi, has already found his younger brother dead, and Stephen (the British officer) has just held a dying comrade. The German soldiers work valiantly to open a space for the trapped comrades who may still be alive. Stephen struggles to get out, yelling to the men who may free him, but he does not know that it is Germans who will be his rescuers. Then Stephen meets Levi:

> He looked into the face of the man who stood in front of him and his fists went up from his sides like those of a farm boy about to fight. But, exhausted, conflicted, "his scalding hatred of the enemy" deserted him: His arms, still raised, begin to spread and open. Levi

looked at this wild-eyed figure, half-demented, his brother's killer. For no reason he could tell, he found he had opened his own arms in turn, and the two men fell upon each other's shoulders, weeping at the bitter strangeness of their human lives.[6]

In this story, hate drained away in exhaustion and grief, but the hate generated by war is sometimes slow to dissipate, and those who maintain a respect for their enemies may be strongly criticized. At Oxford, Warden Spooner was criticized for including the names of three German soldiers in a memorial list of graduates who died in World War I. He was generously and reflectively right when he said that "to carry on a spirit of hate against those who passed into another world can make us neither better patriots nor better men."[7] Students should hear and discuss this story. Why hate? Perhaps relinquishing hate encourages the question: Why did we fight in the first place? (Note: Spooner might be remembered in English class as the person who made famous the speech error known as a *Spoonerism*: "the queer old dean" when he meant to say "the dear old queen.")

In World War II, hatred for the Japanese ran rampant among American servicemen. Not many Japanese soldiers tried to surrender, but the few who did were often shot down, and the wounded sometimes had their throats cut. Peter Schrijvers writes:

> Rampant rage failed to be extinguished even by orders from above. In a desperate effort to obtain prisoners for intelligence purposes, the Americal Division had to encourage its soldiers with the award of a case of beer or a bottle of whiskey for each Japanese captured alive.[8]

Certainly racism was involved in the American hatred directed at the Japanese, but the Japanese were also guilty of racism:

> A Japanese novelist said he was "itching to beat the bestial, insensitive Americans to a pulp." One publication described the "bestial" enemy as demons, devils, fiends, monsters, and as "hairy, twisted-nosed savages." … Another magazine said of the Americans, "the more of them are sent to hell, the cleaner the world will be."[9]

Ignorance and real differences both played a role in the excesses of Japanese–American racism. Apparently it is easier to hate people about whom you know little and who are of a different race. As we saw earlier, evolutionary biologists have provided evidence that altruism and fellow feeling are most often expressed toward those genetically related to us. In wartime, racial differences and geographic distances are aggravated by psychological distancing. We are too often ready to believe ridiculous reports about people who are not like us. Current educational efforts to help students understand and appreciate other cultures may reduce this form of hatred, but it still seems easy to arouse, and not only among those who have limited education. Military commanders and trainers experience contradictory beliefs and feelings about this. To be effective fighters, must soldiers hate their enemies or, at least, have contempt for them? Does it relieve moral guilt to believe that the enemy is not like us – perhaps not fully human? Should soldiers be discouraged from using disparaging terms to describe the enemy? If hatred, rage, and a disposition toward cruelty fade at the cessation of hostilities, what psychological help must be offered to veterans who now view their wartime rage as a deep moral failure?

Hatred is often induced by war and sustained in civilian populations by propaganda and patriotic fervor. But the cruelty and violence of war are not always products of hatred. Consider the attitudinal differences in American soldiers toward the Japanese and later toward the Vietnamese. Hatred of the Japanese was maintained in part by the belief that it was deserved; the Japanese bombed Pearl Harbor, and they seemed determined to fight to the end. Although much of the cruelty exercised against Japanese soldiers was criminal or nearly so, American soldiers felt justified because they were defending their country against aggression. In Vietnam, the violence and cruelty were often senseless, aimed at a poorly defined enemy, in defense of an equally poorly defined ally. Horrible acts in Vietnam were not so much acts of hatred as of rage, guilt, and desperation. As we saw in the discussion of berserkers, men occasionally engaged in acts that violated their own moral code. It was as though some stranger, residing temporarily within them, had performed the acts. Why did I do that? is a question asked again and again by Vietnam veterans.[10]

Hatred is sometimes episodic in military men. They may feel something like hatred at the start – a feeling stirred up in them, as in civilians, by political contrivance. It may fade away, lost in fatigue, cynicism, fear, and confusion. Then it may arise again in response to the death of a comrade or a painful wound. For exhausted, thoughtful men, it may disappear entirely, to be replaced by a feeling of hopeless compassion for fellows on both sides of the battle. We hear this in the poetry of World War I, in *All Quiet on the Western Front*, and in *Birdsong*.

There are, of course, people whose personalities have become warped – often through childhood abuse – and they are ready to hate almost everyone.[11] In the military, such people are dangerous to both the enemy and their own comrades,[12] and it would take expert therapists to provide them with any chance of healthy lives. Then there are those who, without hate, just enjoy killing. Recall the Union soldier who described killing Confederates as play and J. B. S. Haldane, who enjoyed the opportunity to kill.[13] Most men, however, fall into neither of these deplorable categories.

Educators could provide some psychological protection for young people by giving them the information they need to gain some self-knowledge. We can't immunize young people against the dangerous myths of patriotism and war's glory, but we can prepare them far better than we do now. They should know how their beliefs and attitudes can be manipulated, how they might lose their moral identity, and how they may later be overcome by feelings of guilt and betrayal.

## LONG-STANDING HATREDS

We know from biological studies that human beings tend to defend and support those genetically closest to themselves, and living close together in cities tends to encourage solidarity against threatening outsiders. But living in the same city (or section of the city) may not remove all signs of distrust and dislike. Ignorance and distrust of different groups may exist for centuries and only occasionally flare up into violence. Norman Naimark describes the deplorable practice of twentieth-century ethnic cleansing, for example, as "a profoundly modern experience, related to previous instances in the twentieth century but not strictly speaking a product of 'ancient hatreds.'"[14] It is apparently not simply long-standing hatred that produced the genocides and ethnic cleansings of the twentieth century. Rather, these events were tied closely to something in the times at which they occurred. Naimark points to modern racialist nationalism as one critical factor and to the high technology of such states as another enabling factor.

It is almost impossible to imagine non-Jews in a small village – Jedwabne, Poland – horribly murdering their Jewish neighbors without the poisonous climate established by the Nazi extermination program.[15] Even given that climate, such acts are inexplicable. Poland had been the site of pogroms over a long period of time. One could argue, then, that there was a tradition of distrust, if not hatred, in Poland. In Jedwabne, however, Poles and Jews seemed to be on good terms before the German invasion. Fifty years later, for example, one elderly inhabitant described relations thus:

> Here there were no such big differences in opinion or whatever, because they were, in this little town, on good terms with the Poles. Depending on each other. Everybody was on a first-name basis, Janek, Icek.... Life here was, I would say, somehow idyllic.[16]

How could people supposedly living an "idyllic" existence turn on their neighbors with such violence? Hundreds of Jews (perhaps as many as 1,600) were stoned, knifed, beaten, drowned, or burned to death by neighbors. With a few exceptions, neighbors who were not actively engaged in the violence stood by silently watching. It is perhaps not surprising that the Polish government and people tried for years to deny or ignore the crimes at Jedwabne. Perversely, guilt for such atrocities can deepen hatred for the victimized group. Jan Gross raises the interesting psychological question of whether repressed guilt might be the best explanation for the postwar Polish anti-Semitism.[17]

Gross also asks another question that should be of paramount interest to educators:

> Can one, as a group with a distinctive collective identity, be at the same time a victim and a perpetrator? Is it possible to suffer and inflict suffering at the same time? And he answers the questions: In the postmodern world the answer to such questions is very simple – of course it is possible.[18]

We know, of course, that a great amount of criminal violence is a result of abuse suffered by the criminal.[19] Willard Gaylin, commenting on Gross's book and journalistic accounts of it, discounts the notion that the Poles who killed Jews in Jedwabne did it "because they could." Clearly, Gaylin is right when he insists that we need a more convincing account of their motivation: "All of us have the opportunity to torture animals, but the majority of us do not. We are disgusted and bewildered by that minority that takes pleasure in doing so."[20]

The criminal Poles, it seems, saw themselves as victims of one recent conqueror after another and, perhaps, as long-term victims of Jewish pride and distinction. Sometimes perpetrators really are victims (as in the case of criminals who suffered childhood abuse), and sometimes they merely perceive themselves to have been victims. The latter case can be even more destructive than the former, because the perpetrators, subconsciously aware of their guilt, may nurture continued hatred and resentment for decades. Apparently, some persecutors of Jews experienced renewed hatred because of what the Jews "made them do."

Poland suffered through successive occupations, and it is understandable that some people tried to accommodate whoever was in charge – even when it was obvious that one set of conquerors hated the other. Some became perpetrators of violence to protect their own interests, some out of genuine hatred for the earlier invaders (the enemy of our enemy is our friend), and some because they had simply lost control. Gross notes that totalitarian regimes tap into the usually hidden evil instincts of people. Quoting Eric Voegelin, he writes:

> [Such regimes demoralize] the simple man, who is a decent man as long as the society as a whole is in order but who then goes wild, without knowing what he is doing, when disorder arises somewhere and the society is no longer holding together.[21]

This strikes me, as it might Gaylin, as insufficient. Not all "simple men" go on wild rampages when societal order breaks down. It is understandable that Poles – themselves victims of both German and Russian invasions – might lash out at innocent others, but not all Poles did this. What explains the restraint of most Poles? It is also understandable (but not excusable) that, after their murderous rampage, they would try to shift blame to the German occupiers. The Nazi regime facilitated the murders by establishing a climate of hate and violence, but that still does not explain the bestiality of the rampaging Poles.

What should young people study, discuss, and reflect upon to avoid such tragic outcomes? As part of educating for self-knowledge, educators should give students opportunities to hear stories of the Holocaust and how ordinary people have done horrible things. They should also hear stories of the few people who, at the risk of their own lives, maintained their moral identities and acted to save the lives of victims.[22] What supports such steady, courageous behavior?

Perceived differences remain fundamental in generating and renewing hatred. When, within a society or nation, the group perceived as different begins to thrive economically, hatred may be increased by envy. This was certainly the case with Armenians in the Ottoman society and with Jews in many countries. Although such minority groups may be allowed by ruling governments to prosper, they are often subjected to discrimination – higher taxes, limits on the amount of land they can own, and exclusion from high governmental offices. Difference is perceived and sometimes even encouraged by minority groups themselves who insist on emphasizing their difference in dress, manner, and ritual. Again we find ambiguities in both majority and minority group attitudes. The minority group may want acceptance, but it may also take pride in its difference. The majority group may exaggerate and disparage the differences but also press the minority to assimilate. They want to be sure that, if outsiders threaten, their "different" neighbors will be on their side. In times of international trouble, the majority may – without evidentiary justification – express distrust of their minority groups. Consider the shameful treatment of Japanese American citizens in World War II.

Jonathan Glover also challenges the "ancient hatreds" account and points out that some tribal hostilities are recent.[23] Yet perceived difference – physical, economic, religious – is implicated. In the case of Rwanda, the Hutu government promulgated "information" about the wickedness of the Tutsis. The propaganda was relentless: "[The Tutsis] planned to enslave the Hutus; they were dishonest; they should be excluded from business, education and public life."[24] The ensuing slaughter is still hard to imagine. As in the case of Jedwabne, we have to ask: How could people kill and maim their neighbors? Education should surely play a mitigating role here. All children should be helped to understand the power of propaganda and the need to think critically about social/political issues.[25] It isn't a matter of merely educating, however. The generation that included the Nazis was possibly the best-educated generation the world had yet produced. But perhaps we should not define education in terms of mere knowledge of facts – literary, historical, philosophical, mathematical. The world needs critical education aimed at knowledge of both self and the groups to which one belongs. And that education must be committed to producing reflective, dedicated, moral people.

Sometimes governments or ruling groups decide that physical (geographic) separation is a way to reduce hatred or, at least, the violence it generates. Even if no physical violence is threatened, separation may be advocated in the name of justice. Edward Casey discusses the disastrous effects of a well-intended effort to separate the Navajos and Hopi by relocating some of the Navajos:

> A quarter of those relocated have died, including an unusually high number from suicide.... What is striking in the Navajo tragedy ... is the explicit acknowledgment by relocated people themselves that the loss of land was the *primary* loss – to take the land is to take away life.[26]

The loss of land referred to here is not so much a loss of property, of ownership. It is the separation that hurts so much. The Navajos believed that the mountains could somehow feel that their people had deserted them. Separation under these conditions cannot be recompensed. Like the loss of a parent or child, such separation represents a permanent loss.

The forced transfer of Germans from Poland and Czechoslovakia at the end of World War II is another case of trying to avoid difficulties with little consideration for those who would suffer. Churchill is quoted as saying: "For expulsion is the method which ... will be the most satisfactory and lasting. There will be no mixture of populations to cause endless trouble as in Alsace-Lorraine. A clean sweep will be made."[27]

The expulsion was a horrible episode in "peacemaking":

> The Nazis themselves were the primary cause of spiraling nationalist resentments. In some fashion, then, it is fair to say that the Germans reaped what they sowed. That so many lives were lost and ruined in the ethnic cleansing of the Germans from East Central Europe should be attributed, in the final analysis, to the hatred wrought by Nazi policy in the region.[28]

But, of course, many of the Germans were neither Nazis nor Nazi sympathizers, and they were – as most of us are – attached to their homes and home-places. They were nevertheless tainted by the Nazi connection. Those perceived as victimizers became victims.

The outstanding example of long-standing hatred is anti-Semitism, and it suggests the need for further thought on the influence of ancient hatreds. At the end of his comprehensive and endlessly shocking study, Robert Wistrich writes:

> Since World War II and the Holocaust that decimated two-thirds of European Jewry, it has become impossible to ignore the role and importance of anti-Semitism in the past and present. Hatred of Jews, as we have documented throughout this study, has been an astonishingly resilient and persistent phenomenon throughout the ages ... for all the unprecedented radicalism of German techniques of mass murder, there were deep historical roots to the Nazi hatred of Jews. Hitler's anti-Semitism did not come out of nowhere.[29]

Any reasonable, compassionate person reading this history would find himself or herself agreeing with those who vow "never again." But that vow must be extended to all those who have suffered. We must be concerned, for example, with the Palestinians now, and thoughtful Israelis should (and many do) remember that victims can become victimizers.

The world too often stands by and allows terrible slaughters to occur. Overemphasis on national autonomy is one factor in this negligence. Another is our insistence on calling all armed intervention *war*. In the contemporary world, war demands a justification in terms of national interests, and the engagement of young people in armed conflict requires a devotion to patriotism. The world's leaders must face the need for effective, fully justified police actions. Like all police activities at every level, they should be carefully monitored, but without the rituals and emotions evoked by patriotism, police actions might indeed be conducted justly.

## TERRORISM

Terrorists are often filled with hatred, and yet they want a form of respectability. Louise Richardson writes: "Terrorists want to be considered soldiers at war with an enemy ... the concept of jihad, as invoked by Islamic extremists, for example, is all about war."[30] It is worth noting that it is extremists who speak of jihad as war, whereas many moderate Muslims think of jihad as struggle. Such struggle need not be violent. Michael Bonner says that those who insist that jihad means war and those who see it only as peaceful, individual struggle are both wrong.[31] Historically, it has meant both. But Richardson is surely right when she comments:

Terrorists like to be considered soldiers at war both because of the legitimacy they believe it brings their cause and for the status they believe it confers on them. For the United States to declare war on a bunch of radical extremists living under the protection of an impoverished Afghanistan is to elevate their stature in a way that they could not possibly hope to do themselves. And, too: The language of warfare also induces what Michael Howard has called a "war psychosis." People expect immediate action.[32]

Mark Juergensmeyer also comments on the power inherent in the language of war and warfare:

The idea of warfare implies more than an attitude; ultimately it is a world view and an assertion of power. To live in a state of war is to live in a world in which individuals know who they are, why they have suffered, by whose hand they have been humiliated, and at what expense they have persevered. The concept of war provides cosmology, history, and eschatology and offers the reins of political control.[33]

I will say more in the chapter on existential meaning about the power of war to enliven identity and restore meaning to everyday lives, but here I should note that we would do better to treat terrorists as common criminals, people who have broken the laws recognized by all civil societies. To treat them as soldiers is to increase their power, respectability, and commitment.

While we should pursue and punish terrorists as criminals, we should extend friendship and support to the populations from which they emerge. The idea is to replace hatred with understanding. Hatred is one important motivational factor in terrorism. Several terrorists have voiced their hatred. One accused bomber said:

I hate America because it is the real center of international terrorism, which has already repeatedly tyrannized Islam. I carry out jihad because it is the duty of a Muslim to avenge, so the American terrorists and their allies understand that the blood of the Muslim community is not shed for nothing.[34]

The feeling of being victimized is often a precursor to violence and, as Richardson points out, "The fact that someone who has committed heinous crimes makes allegations against us does not mean that those allegations are without foundation and should be dismissed out of hand."[35] Richardson recognizes that law-abiding nations may use sanctions rather than war to force a rogue nation to comply with international demands. Sanctions are supposed to be nonviolent. However, UN sanctions against Iraq actually caused the deaths of hundreds of thousands of Iraqi children:

> Two successive UN officials in charge of the program resigned to protest the humanitarian catastrophe over which they were presiding. Hans von Sponek explained, "I can no longer be associated with a program that prolongs suffering of the people and which has no chance to meet even the basic needs of the civilian population."[36]

Before von Sponek, Fred Halliday – citing the same complaints – had resigned. He said, "We are pushing people to take extreme positions."[37] It is actions of the sort noted by von Sponek and Halliday that lead some Muslims to declare with some justification that America has been guilty of international terrorism.

The attitude of American exceptionalism noted in the earlier discussion of patriotism aggravates the grievances among people who believe that America intends to dominate the world – if it does not already do so. A change in attitude and tone of conversation is essential here. Instead of insisting on leading, we might genuinely seek partners. Instead of attempting to isolate nations we judge to be offenders, we might increase our connections through student and professional exchanges. And we might admit publicly that we have sometimes engaged in highly questionable acts. It is perhaps too easy – seeing ourselves as the "city on the hill" – to forget the harm and destruction we have caused in Cuba, the Philippines, Korea, Vietnam, Central America, and our own American West. Without descending into self-loathing (which usually triggers further violence), we might participate in global dialogues aimed at understanding, not at blame-finding.

Schools today are working toward global understanding, and much creative effort is going into multicultural education. However, superficial knowledge of others can accomplish little. What is needed is far greater emphasis on self-knowledge. Students should be made aware of how attitudes and beliefs are manipulated in wartime. This is difficult and, if approached directly through specific learning objectives, could rightly be construed as indoctrination and would very likely be opposed by those devoted to traditional ideas about patriotism. There are, however, vast amounts of literature that can be chosen and judiciously discussed. All students should understand what might happen to their moral thinking in times of great stress, and young men who may enter the military right out of high school should certainly be informed about the possibility of losing their moral identity in the climate of fear and rage induced by combat. Indeed, it is morally negligent to withhold this information.

Teachers should be aware that there are hateful personalities – that some young people have been so badly abused that they are ready to hate everyone around them. Such individuals may need more help than teachers can give them. Schools could do much to reduce this problem over the long run by including the study of parenting in the curriculum.[38] It still amazes me that we insist on teaching algebra to all students when only about 20 percent will ever use it and fail to teach anything about parenting when the vast majority of our students will become parents.

In addition to the study of parenting, schools should give some attention to the importance of home and home-places in human life. With a better understanding of how deeply attached many people are to their home-places, we would be more careful about suggesting transfers of populations as the solution to political problems. A "peace" accomplished by separating people from their home-places is a form of violence. We have too often done hateful things in trying to reduce hatred.

Possibly the most difficult problem in reducing hatred is coming to understand the role of difference in generating hatred. Students need to be informed about the evolutionary legacy of human connections along genetic lines and how differences seem to invite distrust. Groups proud of their distinctive differences might, without abandoning their identity, emphasize their common humanity. Today religious differences are perhaps the most likely to cause violent reactions. We turn to that topic next.

# 6

# Religion

Possibly no domain of human thought and behavior is more riddled with ambiguity and ambivalence than religion. Does religion promote peace or does it encourage war? Are some religions peaceful and others warlike? Do religious differences contribute to distrust and violence? Today contention over religion is exacerbated by both the apparent increase in Islamist extremism and the rise of outspoken atheism in Christian nations, and so far, antagonists (believers and unbelievers) have not found an acceptable way to carry on a conversation. This does not bode well for a cooperative program to promote peace.

In this chapter, I will concentrate on the problem of dialogue and, particularly, on what American citizens should know about religious history and thinking in order to converse across the lines of belief and unbelief. The issue is of huge importance for education. I do not suggest that students should be persuaded to adopt either a particular religion or a secular view. I will argue, however, that acceptance of dogmatic views makes rational debate almost impossible and that we must find a way to discuss religion as openly and productively as we do other issues central to human life.

When we think of religion and war today, our attention is likely to fasten on the threats to peace posed by Islamic extremism and/or Jewish orthodoxy in Israel. These are clearly important topics, but I will concentrate mainly on Christianity. How is it that, in a country that describes itself as a Christian nation, Americans cannot study and discuss the varied contributions of Christianity to war, violence, and incivility? Can we make a legitimate claim to *educate* if we refuse to address these issues in our schools?

### THE GOD DEBATE

Some years ago, I wrote a book entitled *Educating for Intelligent Belief or Unbelief*.[1] I was quite sure that public schools would not be permitted to discuss this material, but I hoped that at least a few educators would reflect on the need for such education. I started the book with this sentence: "Intelligent believers and intelligent unbelievers are often closer in thought and spirit than intelligent and unintelligent believers."[2] By *intelligent* I meant well-informed and reflective, and I backed up that introductory comment with similar observations from Michael Novak, Hans Kung, and John Dewey. Surely, I thought, there must be a way for reflective, generously critical people to discuss matters that have long been central to human existence.

Today the educational program I wanted to encourage seems quite hopeless. One reason – important but outside the scope of this discussion – is the current emphasis on narrowly specified information and skills thought to be needed by all students. The concentration on so-called standards leaves little time for the discussion of existential issues and questions that cannot be answered on a multiple-choice test. A second reason, more directly pertinent to the concern about war and peace, is that many supposedly intelligent people on opposite sides of the debate over God and religion are *not* showing any signs of being close in thought and spirit.

Consider the language used by David Bentley Hart in his critique of the new atheism. He opens by noting that Richard Dawkins exhibits an "embarrassing incapacity for philosophical reasoning," but he gives no example of Dawkins' faulty reasoning. He calls Sam Harris's book an "extravagantly callow attack on all religious belief," but he presents no evidence to support his contention that the work is callow. He says that Christopher Hitchens' "talent for intellectual caricature somewhat exceeds his mastery of consecutive logic," and he finishes this regrettable paragraph by declaring that Dan Brown's *The Da Vinci Code* is "surely the most lucrative novel ever written by a borderline illiterate."[3] Such language does not invite dialogue.

Hart follows this introduction with an interesting, well-written (if somewhat questionable) account of the early days of Christianity. He claims no strict objectivity for his account, admitting that it is "very much a personal vision of Christian history."[4] That was fine for my purposes. I was looking for a believer's account to balance the work of the new atheists – work with which I was already very familiar. The quest, in trying to better understand the human predilection for war, was for a model of intelligent, rational conversation on an emotionally laden issue. Clearly, I looked in the wrong place. Toward the end of his book, Hart renews his complaints, and he deplores the lack of "profound unbelief":

> The best we can now hope for are arguments pursued at only the most vulgar of intellectual levels, couched in an infantile and carpingly pompous tone, and lacking all but the meagerest traces of historical erudition or syllogistic rigor: Richard Dawkins triumphantly adducing "philosophical" arguments that a college freshman midway through his first logic course could dismantle in a trice, Daniel Dennett insulting the intelligence of his readers with proposals for the invention of a silly pseudo-science of "religion," Sam Harris shrieking and holding his breath and flinging his toys about in the expectation that the adults in the room will be cowed, Christopher Hitchens bellowing at the drapes and potted plants while hoping no one notices the failure of any of his assertions to coalesce with any other into anything like a coherent argument.[5]

This sort of talk simply increases alienation and a sense of profound difference. I hoped to find a more generous – at least more polite – response to the new atheism from Terry Eagleton in his Terry Lecture. Eagleton's tone is also dismissive, however, and he lumps Dawkins and Hitchens together as though they are one writer he calls "Ditchkins." At least he does address a few of their arguments, and he makes several points on which we might build a useful dialogue across the chasm of belief–unbelief. Drawing on Karl Marx, Eagleton advises:

> Religion needs to be patiently deciphered, not arrogantly repudiated. It springs from a realm to which reason should be no stranger. Only if reason is able to acknowledge the a-rational interests and desires from which it draws so much of its force can it prove sturdy enough to prevent those desires from sliding into anarchy, thus overwhelming reason itself. This is one reason why no polemic against religion pitched simply at the level of rational argument can hope to succeed.[6]

It isn't quite right, however, to say that Dawkins and Hitchens ignore the nonrational interests on which both religion and reason draw.

Indeed, they refer again and again to feelings of longing, fear, ecstasy, and revulsion. That said, it is true that their emphasis is on getting people to think, and they do heap ridicule on a host of religious beliefs. Their point, however, is not simply to put all of life on a reasoned, logical foundation. On the contrary, their main point – made repeatedly – is that religious beliefs too often lead to conduct that does terrible harm, that religion as it has been practiced is *immoral*.

This observation leads to another important point. Both Hart and Eagleton criticize the new atheists for a lack of theological knowledge. They do not say much of substance, however, about this lack, and my own sense is that sophisticated knowledge of theology is irrelevant for the purposes pursued by the new atheists. They are concerned with the usual *practice* of religion and the beliefs espoused by ordinary participants in religious activities. Most members of religious institutions do not know much about theology, and many do not even know the technical doctrines of their own institutions. For example, some prominent theologians do not believe that God is a person with whom one can communicate, but it would be a rare pastor who would espouse such a view. What would the average churchgoer think of Tillich's God above God, or Eagleton's God who is not an entity and is one with the universe, or John Dewey's God as the active relation between the ideal and the actual?[7] Theology is a difficult, fascinating domain of study, but it is unlikely to touch the hearts and minds of those seeking a God with whom they can walk and talk.

Eagleton says that theology can foster critical reflection and mutual understanding, and I think the new atheists might agree, but they are summarily dismissed by Eagleton. He writes:

> Will either side listen to the other at present? Will Ditchkins read this book and experience an epiphany which puts the road to Damascus in the shade? To use no less than two theological terms by way of response: not a hope in hell.[8]

In response, we might ask whether Eagleton has really listened to Dawkins or Hitchens or Dennett.

In contrast to the scornful attitudes taken by both the new atheists and their critics, E. O. Wilson offers a model for reaching out across the chasm. In his book *The Creation*, cast as a letter to a southern Baptist preacher, Wilson (a secular humanist) seeks to enlist the pastor's efforts to save the earth. He acknowledges their differences in clear, everyday terms:

> For you, the glory of an unseen divinity; for me, the glory of the universe revealed at last. For you, the belief in God made flesh to save mankind; for me, the belief in Promethean fire seized to set men free. You have found your final truth; I am still searching. I may be wrong, you may be wrong. We may both be partly right.[9]

Wilson then proposes cooperation on the vital project of saving the creation. If we are serious about saving the earth and ending war, it is this spirit of honest respect that we must cultivate. Even if we disagree on fundamental premises, we may find a project on which we can work together. In doing so, we may begin to listen more respectfully.

Perhaps the greatest barrier between believers and unbelievers is the concept of God's goodness. The God of the Bible and traditional practitioners cannot convincingly be called *good*. Looking at the "horrors and cruelties and madnesses of the Old Testament," Christopher Hitchens asks who "could possibly *wish* that this hopelessly knotted skein of fable had any veracity?"[10] The New Testament, he adds, is not much better in this regard. Earlier, Charles Darwin raised a similar doubt:

> I can hardly see how anyone ought to wish Christianity to be true; for if so, the plain language of the text seems to show that the men who do not believe, and this would include my father, brother, and almost all my best friends, will be everlastingly punished. And this is a damnable doctrine.[11]

The lack of empirical evidence for God's goodness has driven many careful thinkers away from traditional religion. Indeed, James Turner, writing of the nineteenth-century turn away from God, remarked: "Declarations of unbelief often sounded more like acts of moral will than intellectual judgments.[12] The option offered by evolution was taken up by many seeking goodness in the real world. Bertrand Russell, for example, remarked, "The world in which we live can be understood as a result of muddle and accident, but if it is the outcome of a deliberate purpose, the purpose must have been that of a fiend."[13] What sort of "good God" would create a world in which its creatures must eat one another to survive? Several powerful arguments against the goodness of God can be found in Dostoevsky's *The*

*Brothers Karamazov*, in which two brothers – one on each side of the argument – present their cases for and against the goodness of God; they are worth reading.[14] Similar arguments against the idea of an omniscient and all-good God were advanced by both James Mill and his son, John Stuart Mill. The latter wrote of God:

> I will call no being good who is not what I mean when I apply that epithet to my fellow creatures; and if such a creature can sentence me to Hell for not so calling him, to Hell I will go.[15]

If, in opposition to arguments against the goodness of God, someone points to the many charities, educational programs, and continuous efforts dedicated to world peace (and some of these will be discussed in the next chapter on pacifism), nonbelievers can respond that all of these works are products of human goodness and in no way support the notion that God is good. On the contrary, opponents can point to the connection between religion and war and conclude that it might be healthier (more consonant with peace) to put belief in God aside and concentrate on making peace with one another. Can peace-seeking believers and unbelievers work together in the spirit suggested by E. O. Wilson? There are reasons to hope, given the current evangelistic move to emphasize stewardship over dominion.

### RELIGIOUS SUPPORT FOR WAR

The state and religion have long (perhaps always) been intertwined. Augustine recognized the need for religion to cooperate with the state in order to survive. We noted earlier that religion supports the internal stability of nations and states by insisting that citizens desist from killing one another and, at the command of the state, enthusiastically kill designated enemies. Indeed, Diamond names the promotion of religion as one powerful way for government leaders to gain public support.[16] Now and then, religious leaders have opposed particular conflicts but, more often, they have supplied moral purposes to support the state's decision to conduct war. Recall Faust's comment on the argument advanced by some historians that religious beliefs have "enabled the slaughter." She adds, "Civil War Americans themselves would not have questioned what one Confederate chaplain called the '*military power of religion*.'"[17]

In the Judeo-Christian tradition, God himself is cast as a warrior. Jack Miles points out that "Semitic polytheism had divided the roles of creator and destroyer," but "Israelite monotheism required its god to play both those roles."[18] In the Old Testament, God serves as a ruthless commander-in-chief. Gradually, Miles notes, this role changes as the power of Satan is recognized, and God becomes more concerned with wisdom and virtue rather than military prowess and valor. Granted this historical growth, every Christian knows that the military motif remains in hymns such as "Onward Christian Soldiers" and "A Mighty Fortress Is Our God." In World War II, a chaplain was described in song, singing, "Praise the Lord, and pass the ammunition."

When we think of religion and wars, most of us recall a little of what we have learned of the Crusades and what we currently hear in the news about Islamic jihad. Pressed, we may remember studying about religious conflict during the Reformation and the martyrdom of a few heroes who opposed whichever denomination then had control. The Late Middle Ages were soaked in religious violence – not just war, but the torture of heretics and frequent massacres of Jews. The sixteenth and seventeenth centuries saw war after war between Catholics and Protestants, and religious power was exercised repeatedly to persecute women as witches and dissenters as heretics. A long era of religious cruelty slowed almost to a halt with the Enlightenment.[19] Today, it is not uncommon for young Americans to turn away from the bloody history of Christianity and its perceived hypocrisy in claiming to be a religion of peace and seek a more consistent message of peace in Buddhism or some other Eastern religion. However, as Jerryson and Juergensmeyer report, this too is a mistake. They offer examples of bloodshed supported by Buddhists over the centuries:

> All of these cases of bloodshed counter the popular (and also exoticized) notion that Buddhism is an entirely pacifist – and, in this sense, mystical – religion. In fact, ... in regions where Buddhism is part of the ideology of statecraft, there is a pervasive tendency for Buddhists to sanction violence.[20]

Christopher Hitchens also draws our attention to Buddhist short-comings and advises that "there is no Eastern solution."[21] He provides several paragraphs of quotations from leading Buddhist thinkers that show vividly the close connection between state and religion. When Buddhist leaders agree that all sentient beings share in Buddha nature and that all are to be regarded as children of Buddha, some writers conclude that Buddhism is compatible with socialism, others that it requires obedience to a divinely ordained leader – a position closer to fascism. An example of the latter is the support among Buddhists for emperor worship in World War II Japan.

Fair, responsible readers may feel that Hitchens has gone too far when he declares that religion poisons everything. Has religion done no good whatever? But critics of the new atheism also go too far in defending religion. Hart, for example, refers to the "so-called religious wars" of the sixteenth century.[22] He insists:

> No matter how shameful it may have been, all the religious hatred, fear, or resentment of the period taken together was impotent to move battalions or rouse nations to arms, and no prince of the time waged war against another simply on account of his faith.[23]

On one level, this statement echoes that of historians who claim that the violence of ethnic cleansing cannot be traced only to centuries of hatred. There must be something in the present that triggers and sustains violence. But Hart's conclusion that the violence cannot be traced *simply* to religious differences is misleading, even fatuous. Religion was certainly intimately involved in the sixteenth-century wars. It supplied a motive for ordinary people to kill one another at the behest of leaders who may have had other motives. And that is exactly the point argued in this chapter. We are looking for, trying to understand, what contributes to war. Religions have contributed substantially to the instigation and maintenance of war by manipulating and controlling the minds of citizens. Arguing for the elimination of dogma, Bertrand Russell spoke powerfully on the negative contribution of religion:

> I do not believe that a decay of dogmatic belief can do anything but good. I admit at once that new systems of dogma, such as those of the Nazis and the Communists, are even worse than the old systems, but they could never have acquired a hold over men's minds if orthodox dogmatic habits had not been instilled in youth.[24]

Religion is strongly implicated in the phenomenon known as *exceptionalism*. The Israelites claimed that they were God's chosen people and therefore entitled to destroy any enemies unwilling to become their vassals; indeed, they believed that they were commanded by God – the warrior God – to "utterly destroy them."[25] It was also an attitude of exceptionalism that supported the growth of the British Empire – a supposedly generous colonial effort that would Christianize and enlighten backward parts of the world. Notice, again, that one need not claim that Christianity was the only, or even the most powerful, force driving colonialism. It is enough that it was *one* powerful force working in concert with other others. Similarly, the growing power of the United States in 1900 was augmented and justified by the belief that the United States was exceptional – that it was destined by God to be a light to all nations. A reference to "Christianizing" Filipinos helped President William McKinley to acquire the nation's support in occupying the Philippines after the Spanish-American War. As Evan Thomas has noted, "McKinley did not acknowledge, or perhaps did not know, that most Filipinos had long since been converted to Catholicism."[26] And even today, many Americans talk about the United States as the "city on a hill" and claim a right to domination in the name of Christianity and benevolence.

There can be no honest repudiation of the claim that religion has supported war and in many cases instigated horrible violence. The new atheists are clearly right on this. But perhaps there are better answers – more hopeful, more appreciative – to their charges than those vigorous (but largely empty) denials we have examined so far.

### EDUCATING FOR RATIONALITY

Oddly, many scholarly and eloquent theologians have taken positions similar to those of the new atheists. If we read some of the work of Han Kung, Paul Tillich, Martin Buber, or John Hick, we find that, without giving up their allegiance to religion, they express concerns close to those of the most thoughtful atheists. They argue over the personhood of God, over dogma such as the virgin birth, over the existence of hell, over the divinity of Jesus. Most interesting, some even question *theism*, belief in an all-good person-God who is separate from the world yet continuously active in it.

Reading theology is hard work even for those fairly well trained in philosophy, and it would be unrealistic to recommend that high school students read it. However, students can be introduced to some of the problems and the seeming contradictions between theology and the dogma usually promulgated in churches, synagogues, and mosques. Is God continuously active in the world? What evidence can be offered for this contention? If God is all-knowing – if, for example, he knows what we will do even before we act – in what sense can we claim to have free will? Theists believe that God is wholly good. Given the misery and evil in the world, how can this be true? I'll return to this question because answers to it must be considered when we try to find a connection between religion and peace.

The problems associated with theism are so difficult that some theologians and thoughtful believers have simply given up on it. As I noted earlier, several of America's Founding Fathers were deists; they believed in a creator God who, after creating the world, left it to run on its own. This move clearly eliminates most of the problems inherent in theism. But it does not provide a dependable source of personal support, and that is what many people seek in religion. There is no *one* beyond human companions to help us. There is no one to address in prayer.

Paul Tillich has argued the need to transcend theism – to move actively toward the "God above God." Characterizing the age in which we live as one of anxiety over meaninglessness, Tillich advises facing this anxiety squarely and finding the *courage to be* "in the God who appears when God has disappeared in the anxiety of doubt."[27] One might say that this God above God is an active, positive attitude in response to a universe that accepts and encourages our search for meaning.

In a somewhat similar way, Martin Buber has described God as the "eternal Thou." Whenever we meet another, whenever we encounter someone or something in the world and say *Thou*, we are in contact with the eternal Thou. Saying Thou takes us out of the I-It world (the world of objects) and into the world of relation. Buber writes:

> The spirit is truly "at home with itself" when it can confront the world that is opened up to it, give itself to the world, and redeem it and, through the world, also itself.[28]

Theologians are not alone in the effort to retain a faith in God outside of theism. John Dewey also argued that we might profitably retain a sense of the religious while dropping the notion of religion. In *A Common Faith*, Dewey spoke of that faith as

> [t]he unification of the self through allegiance to inclusive ideal ends, which imagination presents to us and to which the human will responds as worthy of controlling our desires and choices.[29]

Dewey goes on to say, "It is this *active* relation between ideal and actual to which I would give the name 'God.'"[30] He adds that he would not insist that the name be given or used. An obvious difficulty with Dewey's view is that one must describe in some detail the ideals deemed worthy. After all, ideologues and political leaders have expressed ideals that seem evil to many of us and to which they are nevertheless committed.[31]

Another, greater, difficulty inheres in all of the attempts to abandon theism and redefine God. It is hard for people brought up in a theistic tradition to give up the idea of God as *personal*, as interested in the private lives and public workings of human beings. One might well ask: Why bother to retain the name *God* for an abstraction? Why not just drop the notion entirely? This is, of course, exactly what is recommended by the new atheists.

There is, however, a long tradition in theology that attempts to defend theism and suggests remedies for its obvious problems. As we noted earlier, many thoughtful, compassionate people have turned away from theism because they could find no evidence of God's goodness. The creation is riddled with pain, wickedness, and misery. Theologians have long tried to explain how evil in the world can be made compatible with God's goodness. This study was given the name *theodicy* by the philosopher and mathematician Leibniz. It is a fascinating study, but it would take us too far afield to dwell on it here.[32] However, one approach to the problem of evil is especially relevant to our exploration of the connection between religion and war; that is the notion that present evil is somehow necessary for eventual peace and good.

Leibniz, following the Augustinian type of theodicy, argued that, if we believe that this is the "best of all *possible* worlds," then "all the evils of the world contribute, in ways which generally we cannot now trace, to the character of the whole as the best of all possible universes."[33] One objection to this approach to theodicy is that it may lead to *quietism*, a resigned acceptance of evil in the world.

An alternative is found in the Irenaean type of theodicy. John Hick gives us a lovely and generous presentation of the Irenaean view – the world as a site of soul-making. From this perspective, evil is not some mysterious necessity in an all-good creation. Rather, it is something to be overcome, and committed believers must work to bring about the good. In doing so, they also build their own souls. This message is found also (in a far less rigorous form) in the work of C. S. Lewis.[34]

The soul-making idea can, however, contribute to religion's support of war, and nations have often waged war "to achieve peace." From the perspective taken in this book, such a claim is highly questionable. The concept of preventive (or preemptive) war falls into this category. The most obvious objection to preventive war is that it can be used hypocritically to achieve purposes that would otherwise not be accepted by a healthy civilian population.[35] Many critics of the Iraq war have raised this objection. The idea of soul-making encourages believers to develop the courage not only to overcome their own weaknesses but also to combat evil in the wider world. The just warrior is perhaps too often and too easily lionized.

In closing this chapter, I want to explore what might be done in schools to inform our young citizens about the connection between war and religion. Bertrand Russell warned:

> Religion prevents our children from having a rational education; religion prevents us from removing the fundamental causes of war; religion prevents us from teaching the ethic of scientific cooperation in place of the old fierce doctrines of sin and punishment. It is possible that mankind is on the threshold of a golden age; but, if so, it will be necessary first to slay the dragon that guards the door, and this dragon is religion.[36]

Russell made an important point, but it must be modified by noting that science, too, has done its share of harm by contributing to war and violence. Caught up in what they think to be a battle against monstrous evil, scientists have worked inventively to produce more and more weapons of violence. Would that cease with the dragon of religion slain?

We should want a rational, moral, and emotionally satisfying education for our children. Working toward such an education, it must be possible to discuss matters at the heart of human existence. I will make a few illustrative suggestions, and I ask readers to consider why they may be (almost certainly *are*) impossible to act upon.

In history and social studies classes, we might include discussions of religion and war in some depth. Looking back, what might have been the purposes of leaders who instigated wars? Why did ordinary citizens think they were fighting? A unit on the history of religious thought should be included. Similarly, as I have argued elsewhere, there could be (*should* be) units on the history of transportation, homemaking, sanitation, and other topics central to ordinary human life, but a rich, nondogmatic study of the connection between religion and war is essential. The inclusion of the aforementioned topics should make it more acceptable to include the discussion of religion, since we can then argue that we are attempting to invite discussion and reflection on all facets of the human condition.

The study of mathematics can encourage religious rationality. In mathematics, students learn (or should learn) that many "facts" depend on axioms – statements that we assume to be true and use as a foundation for a body of knowledge. Take a familiar example from geometry: The sum of the angles of a triangle is 180 degrees. This is true if we accept the parallel postulate of Euclid. If we reject it and substitute an alternative, we can construct two different sets of "facts" representing two very different geometries.

In theology, if we reject a central axiom of Christian belief – one that assumes the perfect goodness of God – we may rid ourselves of the so-called problem of evil. John Hick remarks on the dualism described by John Stuart Mill:

> Thus this form of dualism is capable of being expanded into a comprehensive and consistent position, and one that has the great merit that it solves the problem of evil. But, from the point of view of Christian theology, however, a dualism of this kind is unacceptable for the simple reason that it contradicts the Christian conception of God.[37]

Hick is unwilling to give up the Christian assumption (axiom) that God is wholly good.

Without pressing for any one view over another, teachers could point out that religion (like mathematics) depends on certain assumptions. What sort of theology develops if we reject the postulate that God is all-powerful? Here we can tell the historical story of how Leibniz got into trouble with theologians by suggesting that God – powerful but not *all*-powerful – was subject to the laws of logic. Hence the world in which we live is the best of all *possible* worlds. Some theologians were unwilling to believe that God is subject to the laws of logic. Others have suggested giving up the axiom that God is omniscient (all-knowing), and this had led to an interesting approach to theology in which God knows a great deal but can only see the future probabilistically. Finally, there are those – Carl Jung is an outstanding example – who reject the axiom that God is all-good. From Jung's perspective, God is still learning and growing. Alfred North Whitehead also proposed a process theology. Teachers need not dwell on any of these theological variants. The point is to make students aware that theology, like mathematics, develops from assumptions. In doing this, math teachers have an opportunity to introduce students to the names and ideas of Leibniz, Jung, C. S Lewis, Whitehead, and Hick, as well as Euclid, Riemann, and Lobachesky.

If we are interested in genuine educational change and renewal, we must escape the shackles of strict disciplinary lines and stretch the disciplines from within.[38] We do not need separate courses in the matters that lie at the center of human existence – courses in homemaking, patriotism, friendship, religion, existential meaning, beauty and truth, pleasure, love, war. Rather, we should show that the studies we force upon the young have, in themselves, something significant to say of such matters.

### WHY CAN'T WE DO IT? WHAT HOLDS US BACK?

In this chapter, I have considered how religion has supported war by giving citizens "moral" or "religious" reasons for engaging in violence. I've taken seriously the idea promoted by Bertrand Russell and others that dogmatic religion stands in the way of fully rational and civil debate, and I've invited readers to think about what stands in the way of providing an open and rational education for our young people.

Although the historical record shows that religion has more often than not supported war, there are important exceptions. We turn next to a consideration of pacifism.

# 7

# Pacifism

In the previous chapter, we looked at the long, unhappy history of cooperation between religion and governments in supporting war. However, religions – or more often, religious figures – have sometimes spoken out against war, and some pacifist groups are specifically religious. In this chapter, we'll look at the positive side of religion and offer a brief review of pacifism. The chapter will close with an analysis of the difficulties in putting pacifism into action. As we've seen in earlier chapters, there are widespread, deep-rooted psychological mechanisms working against even contingent or pragmatic pacifism. Unwillingness to include a discussion of these matters in our schools ensures that these mechanisms will survive and maintain a population susceptible to manipulation toward war.

## THE POSITIVE SIDE OF RELIGION

Although I believe that Bertrand Russell was right when he claimed that dogmatic religion stands in the way of giving our children a rational education, I also acknowledge that traditional religious schooling often provides strong moral support for the young. Young people who belong to religious congregations are less likely than their unaffiliated peers to become involved with crime, addiction, gambling, or other vices.[1] Religion clearly makes a positive contribution to the lives of many young people.

I noted in the previous chapter that the theological idea of life in this world as soul-making can contribute to war by emphasizing the need to fight evil directly, and there is a long history in religion of affirming the need to achieve peace through war. But a belief in soul-making can also have the opposite effect. Some who believe deeply are willing to risk their own lives to oppose persecution and violence against the defenseless. Jonathan Glover recounts stories of several church leaders who actively opposed both the Nazi programs of euthanasia for retarded and mentally ill patients and the destruction of the Jews. Some of these courageous religious leaders suffered in the death camps as a result.[2]

Glover states that the loss of belief in a religious moral law should worry even unbelievers:

> The evils of religious intolerance, religious persecution, and religious wars are well known, but it is striking how many protests against and acts of resistance to atrocity have also come from principled religious commitment. [Here Glover gives a valuable list of names.] The decline of this moral commitment would be a huge loss.[3]

I'm not sure he is right on this. Indeed, he follows this statement with a reasonable plea for humanizing ethics, and many of us are trying to do this. Care ethics, for example, does not depend on religion as a source, nor does it accept rationality as the sole base of morality.[4] It is anchored in natural caring, and current work explores ways to extend caring beyond the inner circles of family and local community. Its great strength in the discussion of war is that it does not give mixed messages on the topic. We'll return to this in the last section of this chapter.

There are, however, religious communities that espouse pacifism as part of their religious commitment. The Mennonites, for example, started as absolute pacifists – rejecting all forms of active resistance. In the twentieth century, however, some Mennonite leaders urged that injustice and violence should be actively, nonviolently, opposed,[5] and Mennonites have become leaders in peace movements.[6]

Quakers have long been active in opposing war and violence. The writings of William Penn are still used in today's peace work. As a realistic pacifist, Penn recognized the tie between government and religion and, instead of trying to dissolve or ignore that tie, he worked to increase the nonviolent influence of Quakerism on civil government.[7] A question then arises concerning what that influence should look like. That is another question to which we will return in the discussion of care ethics. A religion or ethic of peace should have a direct and salutary influence on government, but it should not involve converting people to a particular religion. Peace religions such as Quakerism have been careful to avoid doing this.

Religious messages of peace rarely have the power to counteract the more deeply entrenched beliefs connecting religion to patriotism. Sometimes affiliated people accept part of a religion's ideas and reject other parts, and the same is true of members of various organizations working for social justice. Dorothy Day noted with some dismay that many apparently enthusiastic readers of *The Catholic Worker* did not realize that they had subscribed to a pacifist publication. One group wrote to her saying "that they had liked *The Catholic Worker* much better before the pacifists got hold of it."[8] Like schoolchildren, they had heard only what appealed to them. Day commented:

> It struck me then [at the close of World War II] how strange a thing it was; here we had been writing about pacifism for fifteen years and members of two of our groups were just beginning to realize what it meant.[9]

Day and some of her coworkers were inspired by the message they heard in their devout Catholicism, but others among the Catholic Workers were moved more by the perceived need for Christianity to overcome communism. In justifying the latter position, one colleague who had served in World War II insisted that since their enemies refused to use spiritual weapons, Catholic Workers might also have to use more violent methods. Day writes:

> He poses the question – how explain the two thousand years of Christianity during which time Crusades were preached, wars were fought with the blessing of the Church, and warriors were canonized?[10]

Dorothy Day heard and lived by one message from her church; others (most, she admitted) heard quite a different message – one backed up in the history of practice.

It is understandable that many people follow the messages that are most forcibly promulgated, but sometimes people even reword or reinterpret messages that are obviously warlike to make them sound as though they are consonant with a message of peace. In an account of Jewish literature on war, Michael Novak made an attempt to show a resemblance between Jewish principles and Christian just war theory.

As the account is reported, one is struck by the obvious attempt to make war acceptable:

> The principle of war as a last resort is rooted in the biblical injunction, "When you approach a town to attack it, you shall offer it terms of peace" (Deuteronomy 20:10). Peace is the first concern, and war should be the last. Two additional texts (Deut. 2:26 and Judges 11:12) show that peace is always to be pursued before war.[11]

This is the sort of construal that angers the new atheists. How can a nation or army that sets out *to attack* another group claim to send a message of peace? Recall what follows Deuteronomy 20:10 in the next few verses. As noted in the previous chapter, the Israelites are commanded to "utterly destroy" certain groups – the Hittites, Amorites, Canaanites, Perizites, Hivites, and Jebusites. There is nothing on the just conduct of war in this message or anything on proportionality. The other texts cited are similarly misleading. They are not messages of peace. They are embedded in assurances that the Israelites will conquer and destroy enemies under the leadership of their warrior God.

In contrast, there are genuine peace activists among Israel's religious leaders today. Rabbis for Human Rights is an organization that is active in defending Palestinian rights. They acknowledge a double message in their religion. A spokesman for the group, Rabbi Arik Ascherman, is working to uphold his religious values, but he notes that there is powerful opposition:

> In the Middle East, on all sides, the most religious people are sometimes the most hateful. By challenging religious extremism, Rabbis for Human Rights redeems not only Israeli values, but also Jewish ones.[12]

The debate continues, of course, on which groups and individuals are "most religious," which are faithful to the core ideas, which have the blessings of God.

Similar ambiguity and ambivalence are found in Islam. Love of peace is proclaimed, and aggression is frowned upon. "The noted Muslim theologian Ibn Taymiyya [sic] explains that the initiation of attacks on others is only justified when the practice of Islam is being obstructed."[13] But who decides when Islamic practice "is being obstructed"? What looks like obstruction to one sect may be seen by another as mere freedom to practice a different religion or to follow the beliefs of a different sect within Islam.

The word *jihad*, heard so often today in connection with fears of Islamic extremism, is loaded with ambiguity. Historically, it refers first to a body of legal doctrine that is far from settled among Islamic jurists.[14] It also means "struggle" and may refer to a personal or inner battle to become a better person or, of course, it may refer to fighting another group in the name of God.

Comparisons have been made between the concept of just war as it has developed from Augustine and the concept of jihad, although *justice* does not figure prominently in the Muslim concept. Michael Bonner remarks on a feature of jihad that should remind us of similar problems in Christianity:

> Just wars may, of course, be defensive, but they may also, under some circumstances, be offensive: what makes them just is their role in achieving the well-being of the "virtuous city," that association which we all need in order to attain happiness.[15]

But how shall we describe the virtuous city, and can war be justified in trying to establish it? For those of us seeking peace, this notion is uncomfortably close to the notions of chosen people, city on a hill, light to the world, and exceptionalism in general. It may be used to justify war in the name of peace.

In Islam, as in Christianity and Judaism, we find another ambiguity – that between the poor man and the warrior. Charity and compassion are praised on one level but, on another, beggars and the permanently poor are denigrated, and great emphasis is placed on the eventual rewards to be gained by those who give to relieve suffering. In all three religions, those who struggle to change the conditions of poverty are likely to be distrusted; alms-givers are preferred and, to some of those actively involved in the struggle for social justice, this means that government and religion are too often bound together to maintain poverty.

Islam, like Christianity and Judaism, gives guidance to its adherents for the conduct of community life and personal integrity. In every culture, young people guided by religion are likely to experience some moral protection from the vices common in their society. Recall Glover's comment on what the loss of religious commitment might mean at the political/global level. I expressed some doubt about his worry, and I'll repeat that doubt by suggesting that the result will depend on what replaces religious morality. A strong secular ethic might well protect us from ordinary vices, violence, and war.

Buddhist practices also exhibit ambivalence with respect to war. Introducing a book on Buddhist peace work, David Chappell writes:

> Religion touches those intimate levels of the human heart where trust and hurt can lead to either sympathy or hatred. By guiding these responses, religions can inspire either division or reconciliation, war or peace.[16]

The methods practiced by devout Buddhists can lead to inner strength and serenity and to cooperative work for peace.[17] The same steps can be used to develop disciplined warriors and a fighting determination to prevail in both religion and politics.[18]

## PEACE MOVEMENTS

It is astonishing to learn of the sheer number of organizations founded to establish and maintain peace. The World Policy Institute has listed thirteen pages of such organizations in addition to many university clubs devoted to peace studies and another ten pages of foundations that provide funding for peace studies and initiatives.[19] Further, libraries are crammed with books and other publications that study and promote peace. One wonders how it is that wars can continue to be fought when there is so much intelligent and articulate opposition to them. Anyone looking appreciatively at this mountain of work should be moved to ask the questions that motivate this book: What are the psychological mechanisms that support war? What can schools do to reduce their power?

David Cortright tells us that "peace societies emerged in the nineteenth century, but it was only in the twentieth century that peace movements as we presently understand them came into existence."[20] The word *pacifism* is itself a product of the twentieth century. Interested readers should consult Cortright's comprehensive and elegant history. Here I can only touch on some central ideas and continue to press my basic questions.

As we noted in the first chapter, there have been no major wars between developed nations since World War II; the absence of such wars has inspired the notion that we have come to the end of history.

We also noted, however, that there is considerable debate on the issue and, in any case, there are still wars aplenty. Cortright mentions that there were thirty-one wars in 2005 – all of them "armed conflicts within nations between communities divided by ethnicity, language, religion, and/or geography."[21] Wars have not stopped, but they have changed.

We should also note that, although there have been no major wars between nations, the developed nations have not abstained from war. It is especially important for thoughtful Americans to reflect on the record of our nation:

> In the years from 1950 through 2005 the United States used force to attack or intervene in the affairs of other nations dozens of times.... Washington also launched numerous covert actions in which the United States, principally through the Central Intelligence Agency (CIA), sponsored paramilitary forces and engaged in other forms of political and economic destabilization to overthrow or subvert governments and nationalistic movements. This was a record of military intervention in the affairs of other nations unmatched in human history, surpassing even that of Britain during the height of its empire.[22]

In schools, a point about America's military domination might be made by asking students to consider several questions. Where in the United States might we find a French military base? How about a Japanese (or German, Italian, or Arab) base? If students answer that there are no such bases – this is "our" country – teachers might ask them to check out a list of countries in which the United States has military bases. The discussion that follows need neither endorse nor condemn the notion of American exceptionalism. The idea is to get students thinking.

The enormously powerful "military-industrial complex" about which President Dwight Eisenhower warned has continued to grow since 1961, and peace movements have been nearly helpless in curbing it. Watching antiwar marches and protests all over the world in 2002, many of us believed that the "people would win this one" and there would be no invasion of Iraq. Cortright describes the campaign against the Iraq war as the largest in history. February 15, 2003, was "the largest single day of antiwar protest ever organized."[23] The protests were worldwide and were most vigorous in the countries whose leaders seemed to back the United States. The Catholic Church and most Protestant groups condemned the proposed war. Opposition to the war was so strong that the antiwar sentiment was said to be a "superpower." Patrick Tyler of the *New York Times* wrote that there were "two superpowers on the planet: The United States and world public opinion."[24] Even most members of the UN opposed the war, but they were powerless to stop it.

Cortright claims that, although antiwar groups were not successful in preventing the invasion of Iraq, "the peace movement achieved unprecedented credibility and legitimacy."[25] This is arguable. It might equally well be argued that the military-industrial complex is out of the control of ordinary citizens no matter how eloquent and well-informed they may be. We cannot argue that the psychological factors I've been examining *caused* the war. Clearly, economic and political elements operating within the military-industrial complex were responsible for the war. But vigorous opposition to the war did not prevent it, and that opposition faded dramatically once the war was underway. Then all of the factors that support war kicked in, and protests were subdued. Nationalistic patriotism was aroused; our military personnel became heroes; the loss of civilian life was deplored but justified; neighborhoods were destroyed and cultural treasures were ransacked; age-old enmities were rearoused; and the people whose homeland we ravaged were expected to be grateful for the gift of democracy.

It is hard to maintain enthusiasm for nonviolence once hostilities are underway. It is also hard to decide exactly what form of nonviolence should be advocated. Gandhi embraced the concept of *ahimsa* – the refusal to do harm – and his program of *satyagraha* (soul-force) was a form of nonviolent warfare inasmuch as it demanded constant, dedicated action that would inflict no harm. But what is meant by "no harm"? Clearly, physical violence is thereby ruled out. However, it is possible that some nonviolent actions taken to achieve justice may inadvertently inflict nonphysical harm. For example, well-intentioned groups trying to improve the condition of, say, workers in the textile industry may cause considerable deprivation among the very workers they mean to help by shutting down sweatshops. Social history abounds in such examples.

It is also unclear whether Gandhian methods are practical in all situations of oppression. Gandhi, convinced of the power of *satyagraha*, suggested that it be used by the Jews against the Nazis. In response, Martin Buber – who had earlier (1930) written that much could be learned from Gandhi – said that this method could not be used against the Nazis. It is one thing to use nonviolent methods against those who would deprive you of some material benefit, but if their basic aim is to deprive you of life itself, how can you resist nonviolently?

We can draw an important lesson from the correspondence between Gandhi and Buber: It is unlikely that *one approach* can work in all of its particulars in every situation. We must be willing to compromise judiciously, to tinker with the mechanism of a method, and to try something entirely different if the situation does not seem likely to yield to our preconceived mode of solution.

Pacifist peace movements reached a peak of participation after World War I. That unnecessary war, with its horrendous casualty count and tragic outcome, triggered a widespread revulsion to war. At Oxford University, the Union – appalled by the war deaths of so many of its graduates – adopted a resolution stating that future Oxonions would never again fight for king and country. The enormously powerful antiwar poetry written during and after the war was representative of the larger movement opposing war. Thoughtful voices spoke vigorously in favor of the League of Nations and a fair peace treaty. Some even strongly opposed the annexation of German colonies. But imperialism and the desire for vengeance won. Despite the loss of future peace, proponents claim that the peace movement seemed to gain in both stature and credibility.

That credibility was severely strained by the rise of fascism later in the century. The crimes committed by the Nazis delivered a hard setback to pacifists. When Neville Chamberlain, then prime minister of Great Britain, announced that an agreement giving much of Czechoslovakia to Hitler's Germany had achieved "peace in our time," reactions were mixed. Some pacifists held to the belief that almost any concession to Hitler was better than going to war, but world opinion generally expressed disdain for this act of appeasement. And, of course, it did not prevent war. Buber was almost certainly right when he argued that negotiation with the Nazis was impossible. However, the defeat for pacifism was dramatic; pacifism became identified with appeasement.

Appeasement, like any form of bribery, is unattractive and morally questionable when it involves giving away the property of others or putting their lives in danger. However, there are ways of remaining in communication, if not genuine dialogue, to prevent war. Groups that work across international lines should be encouraged to continue their work when peace is threatened. If doctors, lawyers, teachers, tradespersons, artists, musicians, religious activists, and students can continue to talk with one another, citizens in the rogue country will not feel so isolated. Isolation works to consolidate the efforts of those leading a country astray. Isolation virtually assured that German citizens would communicate only with those who were part of the criminal Nazi regime. That's why many of us today oppose attempts to isolate Iran or any other nation that offends large numbers of the world's people. Talking and listening do not necessarily imply negotiation, and they certainly do not mean appeasement. Rather, they represent a moral determination to understand one another and work cooperatively toward a peaceful resolution.

There is another lesson to be learned from World War II. For many people, that war is called the "good war" because it was fought against a regime guilty of unspeakable atrocities. But the Allies did not enter the war to save Jews from extermination. The United States entered the war after it was attacked by Japan at Pearl Harbor and, as a nation, we certainly did not do as much as we should have to save the Jewish population of Europe. The basic question is still with us: Is it right, justifiable, to intervene in a nation's internal activities when those activities include genocide, ethnic cleansing, or some other demonstrable harm to a subset of its people? In the 1930s, Bertrand Russell pointed out that nations would only go to war when their national interests were somehow involved; this was and continues to be the accepted attitude toward war. The hope after World War I and the attempt to create a League of Nations was that some mechanism could be established with worldwide approval that would make it possible for the member nations to intervene collectively in a country's criminal activities without involving war between nations. The League failed, however, and this hope has not yet been fulfilled; despite establishment of the United Nations, national sovereignty still trumps the obvious need to prevent or bring to a halt atrocities committed by national governments.

There is hope, of course, that the United Nations will eventually be strong enough to meet this need. As I argued earlier, an armed force representing international law and order would engage in police actions, not war, and most of the psychological supports for war would thus be removed. But so far, nationalism has overpowered the internationalism of the UN. When the United States invaded Iraq without UN approval and against the expressed opposition of millions of citizens worldwide, it did so out of concern for national interests. That these interests were largely contrived and advertised with considerable dishonesty failed to deter national leaders who had decided to wage war. The peace movement is still alive, but it is no match for the military-industrial complex.

Before closing this section, we should say something about conscientious objection and how it might affect the conduct of war. In 1930, Albert Einstein suggested:

> Even if only two percent of those assigned to perform military service should announce their refusal to fight, as well as urge means other than war of settling international disputes, governments would be powerless, they would not dare send such a large number of people to jail.[26]

However, the increasingly destructive power of technology has made it unlikely that it would matter much if even 10 percent refused to fight.[27] Today the abandonment of conscription in the United States has reduced the need to refuse; one simply does not sign up. There are enough young people who need jobs, seek adventure, or truly believe that they are serving their country to supply the military with sufficient personnel. Lack of a personal reason for refusing military service has turned down the volume on resistance.

Although for centuries there have been men who refused to join in the killing required by war, conscientious objection became important in World War I. Most of the nations of Europe refused to recognize any right of conscientious objection, and the United States limited that right to those who could provide evidence of a sincere religious objection. It was not until the late 1960s that the U.S. Supreme Court ruled that ethical and moral as well as religious objections to war could be used to claim the status of a conscientious objector. The rising number of objectors during the Vietnam War contributed to the abandonment of conscription.[28] The United States has since maintained an all-volunteer military.

In World War II, as we noted in Chapter 1, Robert Lowell refused military service because he believed that, although they had a just cause, the United States and its allies were not conducting the war justly. He objected to the bombing of civilian centers. But objection to particular wars and specific military methods is not recognized as a legitimate form of conscientious objection, even though – as discussed earlier – it has been argued by some that soldiers have a moral duty to refuse to serve when immoral wars or military practices are chosen.[29] Such recognition might render a nation nearly helpless to conduct modern warfare. But again, without conscription, few with such scruples would join the military.

## GIVING PACIFISM A CHANCE

Pacifism has been a conceptually adaptive movement. The idea that no force of any kind should be used was for the most part abandoned in favor of nonviolent activism. But even to oppose all violence has proved to be unrealistic. Almost all peace lovers admit that they would fight to defend themselves and, even more certainly, their children. Buber was surely right when he said that Gandhi's *satyagraha* would not succeed against the Nazis. There are few absolute pacifists. We now more often hear of conditional, pragmatic, relative, or contingent pacifism.[30] It might be best to drop the term pacifism entirely and just speak of peace movements or working for peace.

It should be unproblematic to present material on pacifism or peace movements as history in our schools, and yet it is rarely done as part of history or social studies courses. Indeed, although material on peace education has proliferated, little has been done with it in schools. The last chapter in this book will explore a range of possibilities for a vigorous program in peace education.

Here I want to consider one set of problems associated with teaching about pacifism. Even to include the history of pacifism – an inclusion that seems unproblematic – may encounter resistance. Teaching "about" is often construed as teaching "for" and, in fact, that might happen. Teachers who are devoted to a religion or a way of life might have great difficulty presenting such material in a neutral fashion. Recall the discussion in the previous chapter of Bertrand Russell's comments on how dogmatic teaching impedes genuine education. I remarked there that Russell seems to overlook the fact that science has contributed a great deal to war and violence, and people well trained in science are sometimes not entirely rational and are even dogmatic. We have to find a way to teach reflectively, not just scientifically.

John Dewey, a strong proponent of rationality and the scientific method, nevertheless abandoned his pacifism and supported President Woodrow Wilson's decision to enter World War I. He seems to have sincerely believed that the war would make the world safe for democracy. As the leading philosopher of democracy, Dewey got caught up in what might be called the *one big idea* syndrome. He couldn't seem to see that other things were at stake and that attempting to advance democracy through war contradicted his own views on democracy. He also failed to foresee the way Americans would behave toward German American citizens and antiwar activists. Robert Westbrook writes: "Dewey also assumed as real the rational public that was a regulative ideal of his social theory – an intelligent, democratic community immune to manipulation in the name of 'nationalistic patriotism.'"[31] He was taken entirely by surprise – Westbrook says that he was "somewhat bewildered" – by the irrationality and nastiness evoked in his fellow citizens as they supported the war.

Students should learn about the undemocratic and hysterical behavior of the American citizenry in World War I – even at universities – but they should also learn that people can be blinded by ideals other than the religious. Russell was right about the dangers of dogmatism; Dewey would have agreed. But dogmatism is not confined to religion. Dewey was uncharacteristically unprepared for the behaviors that appeared in the country he considered rationally democratic.

Dewey recovered his open-mindedness after the war and became a strong advocate of intelligent or pragmatic pacifism. As part of peace education, Dewey recommended that history and geography be taught with an emphasis on international, not national, interests.[32] He hoped that schoolchildren, properly taught, would be less susceptible to feelings of hatred and suspicion. It is useful to refer to his contributions to peace education, but it is equally valuable to recognize and reflect on his unfortunate lapse in judgment. Dogmatism can plague secular thought as well as religious thought.

Any mode of thought that lays out complete and final answers to great existential questions is liable to dogmatism. A great attraction of care ethics, I think, is its refusal to encode or construct a catalog of principles and rules. One who cares must meet the cared-for just as he or she is, as a whole human being with individual needs and interests. We might want to say: Well, isn't that, then, a principle – to meet the other as *one-caring*? If it is, it is an odd principle, because it does not tell us what to do, nor does it spell out precisely and measurably what it means to be one-caring. At most, it directs us to attend, to listen, and to respond as positively as possible. (Much has to be said, of course, about what this means.) Because the ethics of care has naturalistic roots, it recognizes that virtually all human beings desire not to be hurt, and this gives us something close to an absolute: We should not inflict deliberate hurt or pain. Even when we must fight to save our children, we must not inflict unnecessary or deliberate pain. This conclusion places us with those pacifists who reject absolute pacifism but hope to come as close as possible to that ideal. Because most of us recognize that we will fight to protect our children, we cannot be absolute pacifists. Our best hope is to work toward the elimination of the factors that encourage war. Care ethics advises us to maintain caring relations and to work hard to restore them when conditions threaten to destroy or undermine them.

Care ethics is concerned with relations and needs. Virginia Held comments:

> The ethics of care calls for the transformation of the different segments of society, with caring values and cooperation replacing the hierarchies and dominations of gender, class, race, and ethnicity.... Instead of domination by military and economic and political power and the marginalization of caring activities, the latter would move to the center of attention, effort, and support. Bringing up persons in caring relations that would be as admirable as possible would be seen as society's most important goal.[33]

The ethics of care emphasizes attention and response to expressed needs, dialogue, and keeping open the channels of communication. By responding to needs, it tries to prevent the anger and resentment that often lead to violence. This does not mean that we must always grant the requests of those who express certain needs. Sometimes we must explain why these needs cannot or should not be met or that we are not the right people to meet them. But we keep open the lines of communication, and by doing so, we hope to better understand both

others and ourselves. Care ethics requires attention to female experience as well as male:

> Not everything should be judged by an established male standard.
> A reevaluation of the entire field of human relations should be
> undertaken to infuse caregiving, diplomacy, global interaction,
> and family practices with an appreciation of the attitudes, skills,
> and understanding described in care ethics.[34]

We will consider further contributions of women's thought on war
and peace in the next chapter.

# 8

# Women and War

There is an impressive history of women's opposition to war but, as in almost every issue treated in this book, there is also considerable ambiguity. Not all women have opposed war. In this chapter, we'll look first at that ambiguity and suggest some reasons for it. Then we'll consider some of the classic literature written by women against war; again, ambiguities will be noted both in that literature and in critiques of it. In the last section, we'll review feminist literature that extends the discussion of peace beyond the cessation of war to the environment of family and community.

## WOMEN'S SUPPORT OF WAR

Women have often supported war, sometimes actively cheering the fight on, sometimes passively accepting that they have no real choice but to support their men in a decision for which many of them have had similarly little choice. The allure of nationalistic patriotism captivates women as well as men. Although, until very recently, women could not participate in combat, they have struggled with the "honor" of becoming Gold Star Mothers.

Traditional descriptions of masculinity and femininity have aggravated the male tendency to violence. Traditionally, women – "true women" – have been expected to support men in upholding a code of honor dedicated to "God and country." Jungians have sometimes represented an extreme in their description of femininity and masculinity. Esther Harding, for example, tells the illustrative story of a soldier who is due to report to his regiment but is induced to remain with a woman he loves. She uses her sex appeal to get him to stay with her "when his duty or honor call him away."[1] Harding finds this act reprehensible, commenting, "All true women blame the woman who acts this way, rather than the man," and she follows up by saying, "A woman who truly loves her man feels under an obligation not to tempt him by her feminine charm, but to safeguard his honor."[2]

Most contemporary Jungians have given up the notion of absolute archetypes and of religious essentialism.[3] Feminist thinkers have condemned essentialism with some vigor. But, as so often happens, writers on opposite sides of the issue have sometimes taken extreme positions and failed to give defensible, nuanced arguments. When essentialism is cast in biblical terms describing women as second-thought creations designed to help men (especially in procreation), women are right to reject it entirely. Indeed, every rational person should reject it. Similarly, the gender archetypes offered by Jung are too contrived and perfect, too sharply separated from the practical world.

But it is not rationally defensible to deny all elements of essentialism. Human beings are biological organisms, and we are affected by evolution. There *is* something called *maternal instinct*, and it has heavily influenced the development of what might be called *cultural evolution*.[4] It would indeed be remarkable if millennia of caregiving experience had not endowed women with some interpersonal aptitudes not widely developed in men. Further, evolutionary biology has presented convincing evidence that males tend more naturally than females to violence.[5] None of this can be used to judge the next individual we meet. There are exceptions, and cultural evolution will undoubtedly produce more of them.

Our biological nature reveals both strengths and weaknesses. Women who seek peace should be warned by the recognition of maternal instinct that we will fight vigorously to defend our offspring. Absolute pacifism is, for us, unrealistic. But we are informed by reflection induced by the recognition of maternal instinct that other women also cherish their children and that we should work together sympathetically to reduce the risk of violence. Similarly, men should be warned by the knowledge of evolutionary biology that the tendency to violence is embedded in their nature. It has been transformed – reclothed really – into warrior virtue, glory, self-sacrifice, and national loyalty, but the elemental tendency is still there. As we have seen, men like Theodore Roosevelt and J. B. S. Haldane have glorified the tendency.

Without denying our biological proclivities, we can still question the cultural construction of masculinity and femininity. Jungians have argued that masculine and feminine traits complement one another, but complementarity can work for either the benefit or the destruction of humanity. When women submit passively to support their warriors, they contribute substantially to the continuation of warfare.

Some of the criticisms feminists have directed at Jungians have also been made of care theorists. Laura Duhan Kaplan, for example, argues:

> By adopting a strict dualism between feminine and masculine development, the theory may *reinforce* rather than overcome the patriarchal dualism that constitutes the self by devaluing the other.[6]

First, it is fair to say that a "strict dualism" between feminine and masculine development might indeed have this effect. But care theory does not posit such a strict dualism. It argues that there is much to be learned and put to practical use by a critical examination of female experience, and it attempts to use the "language" of the mother as contrasted with that of the father. In both languages, careful thinking should be employed. "Whatever language is chosen, it must not be used as a cloak for sloppy thinking."[7] Sara Ruddick does a beautiful job with this, arguing cogently for peace, using expressions such as "love's reason," "preservative love," "fostering growth," "maternal nonviolence," and "histories of human flesh."[8] What we are arguing in care theory is for attention to differences in experience and language, not in essential nature, but some of us do recognize differences documented by evolutionary biology; that is, we accept a bit of essentialism. I do, for example, and I've used those differences to describe two different paths to morality.

In some agreement with Kaplan, other liberal feminists have suggested that care ethics might undermine their quest for equality in the public world by putting great emphasis on women's role as caretakers.[9] But that fear represents a misunderstanding that equates *caring* with *caretaking* or *caregiving*. Caring is a moral way of being in the world, of responding morally to living others; caregiving is a set of tasks that can be done with or without caring. Kaplan is mistaken when she worries that care ethics establishes "care taking as a model of virtue."[10] We are reluctant even to call caring a virtue, although we recognize its regular exercise as virtuous. I have described caregiving as the incubator of care, and I believe that is true. It is largely through direct caregiving that we learn the attitudes and skills required in caring, and the experience is valuable for both males and females but, like all potentially valuable experiences, it does not lead inevitably to caring.

The point is not to elevate caregiving above all other human activities but to acknowledge its foundational role and trace its development in care ethics. It is also to acknowledge the value of caregiving in its own right and to improve the status of caregivers in our society. Accordingly, we might encourage boys as well as girls to consider careers in early childhood education, nursing, elder care, and social work. The low value placed on caregiving is not so much a judgment of the work as it is a result of its identification with women. It is women who have been devalued, and that devaluation has been extended to their work.

The fear that care ethics will send women back to the kitchen and the nursery is ill-founded. With liberal feminists, we want to expand, not narrow, women's opportunities and choices. But whereas liberal feminists put great emphasis on elevating women's status in the public (male) world, care ethicists want to *change the world* and acknowledge the contributions of both female and male experience. In this attitude, we are largely in agreement with Virginia Woolf, who also warned that the world constructed by professional men is not all good. Her words will introduce the next section.

### WOMEN AGAINST WAR

Woolf was asked what might be done to prevent war. In a long and fascinating response, she explored several possibilities – one of which involved opening opportunities for women to enter the professions and play a more active role in public affairs. Woolf wanted to do this to advance the status of women, but she doubted whether this move would help to prevent war. She described the plight of educated women – caught "between the devil and the deep sea":

> Behind us lies the patriarchal system; the private house, with its nullity, its immorality, its hypocrisy, its servility. Before us lies the

public world, the professional system, with its possessiveness, its jealousy, its pugnacity, its greed.... It is a choice of evils. Each is bad. Had we not better plunge off the bridge into the river; give up the game; declare that the whole of human life is a mistake and so end it?[11]

(Unfortunately, about three years after this was written, suffering from recurrent depression, Woolf decided to end it; she committed suicide by drowning.)

Woolf was stymied by the ambiguities revealed in her analysis:

For reasons given above [on women's work in the professions] we are agreed that we must earn money in the professions. For reasons given above these professions seem to us highly undesirable. The question ... is how can we enter the professions and yet remain civilized human beings; human beings, that is, who wish to prevent war?[12]

She is caught in a dilemma. Although she wants opportunities for women in the professional world, she does not want to settle for equality in that world. It is by its very nature, she thinks, supportive of violence. Nor does she have faith in the role of women as self-sacrificing, passive copies of the "angel in the house." This role, too, supports war. So, what is to be done?

She recommends a form of separation and indifference with respect to male warriors. Most readers – feminists and other pacifists – find her solution unsatisfactory. It is in part a product of her depression and in part a product of her careful assessment of women's lives and lack of power. Deprived of full citizenship until recently, lacking a history of professional accomplishment, and with few roles in political life, women have had little choice but to copy Lysistrata and withhold all attention to male warriors. She recommends that women not only refuse to fight but also that they maintain "an attitude of complete indifference" toward everything involving fighting and masculine honor. Far-fetched as this sounds – depending for its effectiveness on the actions of individual women – there are some powerful ideas in Woolf's essay.

Consider what might happen if we urged (or even allowed) school-children to adopt Woolf's attitude:

[The indifferent woman] will bind herself to take no share in patriotic demonstrations; to assent to no form of national self-praise; to make no part of any claque or audience that encourages war; to absent herself from military displays, tournaments, tattoos, prize-givings and all such ceremonies as encourage the desire to impose "our" civilization or "our" dominion upon other people.[13]

Woolf understood that opposition to war must be pressed at the level of psychology. But how shall we talk about it? Should we speak of campaigns, battles, struggles, protests, fights? Woolf answers a male correspondent who wants to get rid of war:

> [W]e can best help you to prevent war not by repeating your words and following your methods but by finding new words and creating new methods.[14]

She was right, but we are still looking for those words and methods. Her despondency haunts us even today. As mentioned earlier, Sara Ruddick has made a good start in introducing new words into the discussion of peace, and we will look further at her work.

Jane Addams took a different approach to the prevention of war. She, like Woolf, was cosmopolitan in her outlook, but she did not embrace the role of outsider – a person resigned to working alone in dedicated indifference. Rather, Addams met with political leaders all over the world and worked tirelessly with organizations before, during, and after World War I. She worked with the Women's International Committee for Permanent Peace and helped it to develop into the Women's International League for Peace and Freedom (WILPF), which is still active today.

I mentioned in the previous chapter the bewilderment experienced by Dorothy Day when it became clear that many regular readers of *The Catholic Worker* seemed to have no idea that it advocated pacifism. It would seem that pacifism can be attractive (or a matter of indifference) when there is no threat of war, but when war occurs, pacifism is often equated with lack of patriotism, disloyalty, and even treason. Addams, whose reputation for her work in educating immigrants, relieving poverty, improving urban neighborhoods, and advocating an international outlook was stellar, suffered widespread abuse when she opposed the entry of the United States into World War I. Unlike John Dewey, who gave way and supported the war, Addams stood fast in her opposition despite frequent attacks and misunderstandings that she could not clear up. Her reputation was largely, but not wholly, restored after the war, when interest in pacifism once again became respectable.

Addams was steadfast in both her opposition to war and her defense of democracy. The idea of making the world safe for democracy through war seemed contradictory. Addams was appalled by the treatment of German Americans and resisters during the war. If we were seriously devoted to democracy, we would defend civil liberties – even during war. How could the world be made safe for democracy when the land that thought of itself as the heart of democracy ignored the liberties for which it was supposedly fighting? As noted earlier, Dewey too was badly shaken by the irrational atmosphere of persecution and intolerance that pervaded the United States during World War I. Addams joined cause with those who actively opposed this trend.[15] It is somewhat ironic, then, that when she was awarded the Nobel Peace Prize in 1931, she shared it with Nicholas Murray Butler, who, as president of Columbia University, had summarily fired two prominent professors who expressed reservations about the war.

Addams conscientiously studied pacifism. She visited Tolstoy, expecting to learn more at first hand. Apparently, Tolstoy was somewhat rude and came across as more than a little self-righteous. Addams was always willing to challenge her own opinions and so, even though she doubted some of Tolstoy's dictates, she left the visit determined to engage daily in some physical work at Hull House. She would spend a couple of hours a day in the bakery there. On reflection once at home, she decided against this:

> "The whole scheme seemed to me … utterly preposterous." There were people waiting to see her; there were letters to be answered, sponsors to encourage, meetings to attend, politicians to challenge, and essays and editorials to write. Was everything else to wait as she tried to "save my soul by two hours' work at baking bread?"[16]

This is an endearing confession. Unlike some leading male pacifists, Addams did not make herself into an icon. She was devoted to her causes, not to her own image.

We can learn something from both Addams and Woolf. Addams worked tirelessly and optimistically in the public world (a male-dominated world) for peace. Woolf raised serious questions about that world and the possibility of preventing war in it. Conflicted and depressed, she asked whether women should join the "procession of educated men."[17] Addams worked generously and directly with immigrants and their children; through Hull House she established a model of education that seeks both healthy assimilation and the preservation of original cultures. Woolf asked crucial questions about education and the prevention of war: "What kind of education shall we bargain for? What sort of education will teach the young to hate war?"[18] She gave us some clues, some broad directions. We must do something about *patriotism*, about *masculinity*, about *femininity*, about *pageantry*, about *weaponry*, about hunting for sport. But she had little hope that education would treat any of these topics in a way that might contribute to the prevention of war. On the contrary, education – it seemed to Woolf – upheld and exacerbated the worst features just mentioned.

Now we must ask: Can we somehow combine the psychological insights of Woolf with the political will and commitment of Addams? Feminist thinkers have tried. Following the example of Addams, they have sought greater power in order to exercise more influence in the political world.[19] Betty Reardon, for example, recommends a partnership between men who refuse to fight and women whose main goal is the preservation of human life. They must work together to establish a "truly human society." She identifies two major transformative tasks that must be undertaken if a truly human society is to be constructed:

> achieving equality for women and complete disarmament. Achieving the first task would give social value to positive feminine human traits, and the accomplishment of the second would require denial of social value to the most negative masculine traits.[20]

The difficulty here is one that Woolf saw and wrote so persuasively about. *Equality* has so far been defined as equality in the male-defined world. To obtain that equality – as a central element of it – women must be educated in male-dominated institutions. Birgit Brock-Utne, in agreement with Woolf, sees great danger in this. She warns in particular against women joining the military:

> If we too become men, then there is no hope for humankind. Rather than joining the army we should help men refuse to do military service, refuse to kill. It is too easy to copy men's ways and label it "equality." There has always been a tendency for the oppressed to imitate the oppressor. Women have to counteract

such a tendency. We have to discard as utterly dangerous to the human race all those values developed by men that are based on violence and oppression.[21]

Both Reardon and Brock-Utne see the necessity for raising the value of positive female traits. But Reardon believes, as Addams did, that equality might achieve this reevaluation. The quandary – one that Woolf saw with depressing clarity – is that the process of achieving equality may very well demand the rejection or destruction of the values we seek to elevate. As Woolf put it, we find ourselves between the devil and the deep sea. This observation underscores the necessity of finding ways to modify education that will elevate positive female traits and encourage both girls and boys to hate, not love, war. It will be our focus in the last chapter of this book.

## A LARGER PEACE

Feminist writers have pointed out that peace is often defined by male researchers as simply the cessation of war.[22] But sometimes the cessation of official war is followed by continuing violence. The ethnic cleansing of Germans from Poland and Czechoslovakia at the end of World War II is an example.[23] The forcibly displaced Germans were not living in peace. So long as organized violence continues, there is no real peace. However, we must be careful not to weigh down the concept of peace with too many demands. We seek peace with justice, but sometimes we have to settle for the absence of armed hostilities and conditions under which we can work toward justice. If we insist that there is no peace without justice, we would have to admit – given the continuing subordination of women – that there has never been peace in the world. Thus, although the concepts should be complementary, they are different. Conditions of peace should provide a context for the pursuit of justice; the achievement of justice should help to prevent war.

Women have contributed substantially to a larger conception of peace by examining and discussing the need to eliminate violence in interpersonal relations, families, communities, and the natural world. Elise Boulding, for example, has argued powerfully for a careful and continuing study of families as small societies.[24] The best families provide a model for peaceable societies; a study of the worst may reveal what often goes so terribly wrong in larger societies. Boulding reminds us:

> Family life is an act of continuous creation – the creation of human beings and of the society in which they live.[25]

I will say more about Boulding's analysis of family life in the last chapter when we consider specific recommendations for changes in education, but here we should note – with an awakened astonishment – that, if the family is a nucleus of society, it is quite incredible that it is studied so little in our schools. Where do we study in any depth household management, gardens, child rearing, spatial arrangements conducive to conversation, hospitality, light and air, and age-related development?

Sara Ruddick suggests a powerful alternative to the popular male-dominated approach to peace called *conflict resolution through mutual concessions* (CRTMC).[26] One problem with this method, Ruddick claims, is that it induces a continual struggle for a stronger negotiating position. A second is that it takes advantage of weaker partners who have little to begin with and therefore much to lose in giving even ostensibly small concessions. Ruddick acknowledges that "the weaker are not less domineering than the strong but only people who have not yet gathered the strength needed to retaliate and domineer in turn."[27] This comment reminds us of the disappointment of Paulo Freire when he noted that the oppressed, upon liberation, too often turn around and become oppressors. But Ruddick does not settle for recognition of this phenomenon and disappointment in it. She wants to find an approach that will reduce the struggle for power and advantage.

Her alternative is rooted in relationships and the recognition that "the ideal of equality is a mystifying phantom."[28] She notes that there are many relationships in family life and that they are rarely equal. Power relationships shift, and individuals may be strong in one situation and weak in another. Mothers are in a position to watch and work within these shifting power relations:

> Their own peace-making – their attempt to create conditions of peace – includes training for active, engaged nonviolent fighting. Rather than depending on an illusory state of equality, they aim to fight as they live, within communities that attend to and survive shifting differences in power.[29]

I would add here that the ideal of equality is not only a phantom; acting to realize it may help to perpetuate the undesirable features of those in power. Sometimes, of course, it is good to hold up models of the successful and admirable as forms to be emulated, but too often the models are embraced in their entirety, with an emphasis on the elements most closely associated with power. Equality for women, for example, has meant equality with men, and that means higher salaries, participation in the military, "toughness" in politics, and a deemphasis on hands-on caregiving. Rarely do we consider the possibility of learning from, or emulating, those who are less powerful. As Woolf argued, equality should bring desirable opportunities for women, and we would be foolish to reject them, but joining the procession of educated men seems to suggest that we also join the procession of *marching* men. The hope expressed by Jane Addams and other feminists that women's equality would turn the political balance toward greater social sensitivity, caring, and the prevention of war has not so far been realized.

Ruddick admits that there are "moments of CRTMC" in family life, but they are only moments. In the long run, over time, maternal peacemaking requires staying with, giving, receiving, renewing communication:

> The peacemaker asks herself and those she cares for not what they can afford to give up, but what they can give, not how they can be left alone, but what they can do together.... [T]he task of making peace by giving and receiving while remaining in connection is radically different from and less dangerous than CRTMC.[30]

Carol Adams widens the idea of peace by extending concern to nonhuman animals.[31] Both research and common sense tell us that she is right in warning that violence toward and abuse of animals by children are signs of a disturbance that may bring further violence in adulthood. Men who abuse women often have a history of abusing animals in their earlier years. Although Adams is right in connecting childhood acts of animal abuse to other forms of violence, especially the abuse of women, she goes too far in accepting the conclusions of other feminists who warn that owning a gun and hunting are signs identifying a possible batterer. Not all men who hunt are prone to using violence on their wives and children. Some men hunt to preserve the skills by which their forefathers managed to feed their families, and they use the animals they kill for food. True, it is not necessary today for men in urban America to hunt and kill for food, but neither is it necessary for women to can tomatoes and make their own jams. Still, many of us do it.

Readers may protest: But canning tomatoes is not an act of violence! Killing a deer, partridge, or rabbit *is* an act of violence. Yes, but unless we abstain from meat entirely, someone must kill animals, and many men who hunt accept this responsibility for themselves.[32] Those who decide to become vegetarians or vegans have made an ethical decision for themselves, but the decision need not be construed as a universal moral law.

My concern here is with the recommendation to avoid meat and animal products as part of a solution to achieve a peaceful world. Just as Gandhi's *satyagraha* is not applicable in all situations and absolute pacifism has proved unworkable, universal vegetarianism is not a perfect solution. If we all decided not to eat meat, many animals who now live short lives would have no lives at all. They would disappear from the earth, and so would many of the animals – cats and dogs – that we cherish as pets. There is no perfect solution to this problem. Even if we humans stop eating meat, nonhuman predators will continue to kill and eat other animals; the lion will not lie down with the living lamb. The world is naturally full of blood and misery, and unless we want to join Schopenhauer in rejecting life itself, we must do the best we can with our natural environment. And we *can* do better. We can ensure that the lives of food animals (however short) are safe, comfortable, healthy, and free from pain and fear. We can reduce the quantity of animal products we eat and thereby reduce the air and water pollution created by animal waste. We can stop caging chickens and confining veal calves to cruelly small spaces. We can selectively stop eating meat that comes from animals treated cruelly; we should probably stop eating veal entirely.

Without pressing for an absolute, perfect peace, we can continue to extend the idea of peace beyond the cessation of war. Adams, Boulding, Ruddick, and many others have noted that the family should be a model of peace and peacemaking. Women and children do not live in peace if they are abused; nonviolence must pervade all communities of human life.

It might seem to some that there is a contradiction between Sara Ruddick's celebration of maternal thinking and Virginia Woolf's scorn for the traditional role of mothers, but their views are largely in agreement. Ruddick encourages men to participate in maternal thinking and links this thinking directly to peace in the larger world. Woolf deplores the condition of women in the patriarchal family and sees that arrangement as prototypical of the master–slave relation and of the masculine desire to dominate, but she obviously (if ambivalently) admires the quality of maternal thinking later described by Ruddick. Consider her beautiful portrait of Mrs. Ramsey in *To the Lighthouse*.[33]

Woolf also reminds us "that the public and private worlds are inseparably connected; that the tyrannies and servilities of the one are the tyrannies and servilities of the other."[34] Contemporary feminists have built powerfully on this theme: The private is public. It is no longer acceptable for men to beat their wives (even with a switch of legally accepted breadth) or to rape them. Conduct within households must meet a publicly acceptable standard.

It has become clear that the domination exercised by fathers in the patriarchal family supports the attitude of domination in the wider world. Men created a father-god in their own image and then used that father-god to justify their own tendency toward domination. Men, speaking for the god they created, wrote:

> And God said, Let us make man in our image, after our likeness: and let them have dominion over the fish of the sea, and over the fowl of the air, and over cattle, and over all the earth, and over every creeping thing that creepeth upon the earth.[35]

Much to their credit, many Christians and Jews now reject the notion of dominion and embrace instead a concept of *stewardship* – responsibility to protect and care for the life of planet Earth and all of its inhabitants.[36] This is an important step away from the age-old longing for domination. Matthew Scully ends the lovely book in which he deplores human cruelty to animals and describes the hope encouraged by new attitudes with a quotation from Revelations:

> Perhaps that is part of the animals' role among us, to awaken humility, to turn our minds back to the mystery of things, and open our hearts to that most impractical of hopes in which all creation speaks as one. For them as for us, if there is any hope at all then it is the same hope, and the same love, and the same God who "shall wipe away all tears from their eyes; and there shall be no more death, neither sorrow, nor crying, neither shall there be any more pain: for the former things are passed away."[37]

The passage of love and hope quoted here stands in marked contrast to most of what we read in Revelations, however, and in fact, four verses later, we encounter the usual threats of fire and brimstone, of a second death. And even in its beauty, the passage quoted by Scully goes too far – eliminating all pain, sorrow, and death. If, holding fast to the real earth, we manage to reduce cruelty, pain, and sorrow, we will have accomplished something quite wonderful. Surely, the accomplishment will not be promoted by "the same God" that threatens fire and brimstone, the bloodthirsty warrior so vividly described in the Bible. No. If there must be a god involved, it will be a very different deity.

Feminist theologians and philosophers have written about Goddess worship in an attempt to revive the feminine aspect of divinity.[38] It is, however, not clear that Goddess religion actually protected women from male domination. The historical record does not support a claim that there was a golden age for women when female deities were worshipped. Acknowledging that fact, it can still be rightly stated that male monotheisms squeezed out all vestiges of feminine divinity. Riane Eisler notes:

> If we read the Bible as normative literature, the absence of the Goddess is the single most important statement about the kind of social order that the men who over many centuries wrote and rewrote this religious document strove to establish and uphold. For symbolically the absence of the Goddess from the officially sanctioned Holy Scriptures was the absence of a divine power to protect women and avenge the wrongs inflicted upon them by men.[39]

The tendencies within major religions toward tolerance and stewardship should be encouraged, but religious extremists still represent one of the greatest threats to a wider vision of peace. Women might do well to abandon all institutional religion and pursue peace through the best examples of actual peacemaking available to us in real life. Unfortunately, we are still threatened with hell if we consider doing this.

We have considered how women have supported war and how they have opposed it – another great ambiguity in the human attitude toward war. We have also looked briefly at women's contributions to a wider vision of peace. At bottom, it is clear that war has been a central factor in the human pursuit of existential meaning. That is our next topic.

# 9

## Existential Meaning

Human beings seem to need a deep and dependable source of meaning in their lives. When we speak of existential meaning, we are not talking about looking up definitions in the dictionary. Existential meaning affects every aspect of our being – what we believe, how we treat others, what we love, how we live. In discussing the dominant anxieties suffered by human beings, as noted in the chapter on religion, Paul Tillich has argued that the anxiety of meaninglessness has been the major category of anxiety in modern times.[1] Without meaning in our lives, we experience a feeling of emptiness. The feeling may come and go. Meaning may rise and provide stability, and then it may disappear, leaving us empty again.

In earlier chapters, we have seen that war has frequently been a source of meaning in human lives. It has been supported by religion, patriotism, and the desire to participate in something larger than personal life. But what other sources of meaning have been shut off or quieted when war takes over? Is everyday life without meaning? Is it fundamentally boring? Or is the home so filled with meaning, so precious, that we are willing to fight if we believe it is threatened? We will see that both conditions send people to war.

### EXISTENTIAL ANXIETY AND MEANING

People have always sought meaning in their lives. Sometimes the search is for what Tillich calls an "ultimate concern" – something that will give lasting meaning to one's life and activities – but often it seems to be a scramble among basic values for the one most powerful and relevant to current happenings. Tillich suggests that the anxiety of meaninglessness grew substantially across the Western world with the Reformation and the corresponding reduction in the power of the Catholic church. Life's priorities were no longer neatly arranged by order of church and ruler. Even today, people who believe that the purpose of life is to know and love God may be relieved of the continuing search to find a purpose, but almost certainly, there are now fewer such people.

Along with the reduction of religiously established order, philosophy changed. In the late nineteenth century and increasingly after World War I, essentialist ideas in philosophy came under attack. The idea that the lives of humans could be or should be understood or modeled on the order of the universe was challenged, and human freedom became a major theme. Existentialists talked about the fundamental freedom of consciousness, not political freedom, and debate over the basic nature of self-consciousness or self-awareness continues today. With the recognition of freedom came anguish and anxiety. Reflective recognition of our ontological freedom, Sartre told us, causes anguish to the point of nausea.[2] Uncertainty and an overwhelming sense of individual responsibility clashed with a corresponding sense of powerlessness and longing for meaning.

Even in theology, there was a move toward human freedom and responsibility that carried religious thought beyond theism. Nietzsche declared the God of theism dead, and Tillich advised us to look to the "God above God," a God that is not itself a person, but a source of ultimate concern. Martin Buber, too, warned us that this God beyond theism cannot be described as we describe a human person or object,[3] although he acknowledged that God has the attribute of person-likeness. We meet this God through encounters with other human beings, other living things, and objects in the world when we attend fully in an I–Thou relation. Buber's description of contemplating a tree is a beautiful example of the I–Thou relation. Instead of studying it, treating it as an object, I may be drawn into relation with the tree. God, too, Buber said, may wrongly be treated as an "it." Too often, he said, God is described by men who have created him in their own image, and every such description is necessarily faulty. The existentialist attempt to redefine God has, however, been rejected by most religious people. They want a God to whom they can pray and from whom they can receive a response; they want the God described in their holy books. An abstract God – even one with person-like attributes – does not satisfy the longing for meaning. For those who accept the demise of theism, moral responsibility is even more keenly felt.

In an earlier chapter, we discussed the role of religion in supporting war. With a relative decline in the power of religious institutions in the West, one might predict greater resistance to war. In fact, as we saw earlier, there were protests throughout the Western world against the Iraq war, and mainline religious groups were part of the protest, but the war proceeded despite the opposition. If there had been a draft in the United States, the protests might have been effective. Lacking the draft, the military drew heavily from groups of young people who had not achieved much success in school and, in a major effort to compensate for the reduction in official military personnel, recruited unprecedented numbers of civilian workers.

The newfound sense of freedom from ordained order and dogma has produced both exhilaration and profound anxiety. Like children who find themselves unexpectedly in a permissive household, some of us have been tempted to run wild. Others have attempted to escape freedom by retreating to an inner citadel. Isaiah Berlin describes this move as one that rejects desire and attachment, thereby avoiding loss. Tyrants and natural forces may threaten me:

> But if I no longer feel attached to property, no longer care whether or not I am in prison, if I have killed within myself my natural affections, then he cannot bend me to his will.... It is as if I had performed a strategic retreat into an inner citadel – my reason, my soul, my "noumenal" self – which, do what they may, neither external blind force, nor human malice, can touch.[4]

This, Berlin reminds us, is the way of ascetics, Stoics, and Buddhists.

Most of us, however, continue to live in the real world of social and political forces, and there our task is to use our freedom wisely and justly. No one – certainly not an existential philosopher – claims that the actual, physical individual is totally free; political freedom is still being sought. But the claim of an ontologically free consciousness is asserted again and again. Sometimes we embrace that freedom; sometimes we misuse it; often we seek to escape it.

Existentialism looks closely at life's extreme situations, one of which is suffering. Viktor Frankl, an existentialist psychiatrist, discusses the centrality of suffering in existential philosophy. He goes so far as to assert:

> Existential analysis recognizes the meaning of suffering, instills suffering in a place of honor in life.... Only under the hammer blows of fate, in the white heat of suffering, does life gain shape and form.[5]

His emphasis on the freedom of consciousness leads him to see suffering as an opportunity for free expression. The victims of the Holocaust could not control their physical condition or destiny, he writes, but they *could* choose their attitude toward it. Is this true? I have suggested that Frankl asks too much of sufferers. We cannot know how we might respond if we were faced with the thing we most fear. Someone else might face it bravely, although we cannot; similarly, we might be stoical in a situation that would send another into a panic:

> I think here of Winston Smith in Orwell's *Nineteen Eighty-Four*. Faced with his greatest fear, deliberately inflicted on him by the evil O'Brien, Winston betrays Julia, his beloved, and what he takes to be his most basic human capacity – to choose.... In another situation, one that might seem even more horrendous to others of us, Winston might have suffered nobly.[6]

Too often existentialist thinkers repeat the error of their predecessors by looking for some certain, absolute element or characteristic at the center of human reality. Consciousness, like the whole human person, may search for freedom and even feel its weight of responsibility now and then, but there is nothing certain or absolute about it.

Coming into prominence at roughly the same time as existentialism, behaviorism cast doubt on the notion of freedom. Denying the existentialist emphasis on anxiety, B. F. Skinner wrote:

> Our age is not suffering from anxiety but from the accidents, crimes, wars, and other dangerous and painful things to which people are so often exposed.[7]

Skinner located the causes of human conduct and attitudes in events and conditions in the environment, not in an ontologically free consciousness. Our task, if Skinner is right, is to find ways to control and shape the environment so that all people can live, grow, and achieve the success of which they are capable. But who is to shape this environment? Who should be trusted to provide the sort of control that will make us somehow better? What will become of our "unconquerable soul"? The behaviorists, like the existentialists, may have gone too far.

Both approaches, however, yield insights. There is no question that we are largely shaped by our environment, including our genetic environment, and our autonomy is limited. Even the desire for autonomy is conditioned by our social/cultural environment. In liberal Western culture, great emphasis is placed on autonomy. In other cultures, group identity figures more prominently. That said, we are still creatures who seek meaning. We do seem to have something that might be called *spirit*, a part of us that sometimes soars and sometimes sinks without a discernible external cause. We ask: Is there a purpose to life? How should I live? What good is it? Why am I doing this and not that?

Not everyone feels the need for an ultimate concern, but most of us experience shifting concerns that motivate us very like an ultimate concern. The birth of a child or the death of a parent may create such a concern – one that dominates all others for a significant period of time. Getting married, finding the right job, becoming entranced by an area of study, or committing oneself to a charitable cause can all function as an ultimate concern. They give meaning to our lives.

But not all candidates for the sort of concern that gives life meaning are healthy and morally worthy. Hatred, for example, can provide meaning to some lives. Eric Hoffer writes:

> Passionate hatred can give meaning and purpose to an empty life. Thus people haunted by the purposelessness of their lives try to find a new content not only by dedicating themselves to a holy cause but also by nursing a fanatical grievance. A mass movement offers them unlimited opportunities for both.[8]

When we seek meaning, intellect and affect should be bonded. We may be swept away by feeling, but when this happens we should step back and reflect. If I commit myself to this thing that so powerfully attracts me, what effect will that commitment have on my other concerns? Why am I so attracted? Is there something wrong with the life I have so far lived or is this new direction a fulfillment of sorts?

In its educational function, a liberal democracy shrinks from the sort of manipulation suggested by extreme behaviorism. We do not want to exert too much control over our citizens, and we argue perpetually over how much is too much. Some people do want to define the ultimate concerns for their children and even for their nation, and they believe it is their duty to do so. An education that encourages students to look at things from different perspectives is regarded as undesirable, unpatriotic, and even immoral. At the extreme, such people are fanatics. Others of us want to explore a wide range of possibilities and help young people to understand what they may choose and why. This debate remains at the heart of educational philosophy and policymaking.

UNDER CONTROL

The longing for meaning takes a bad turn when it fastens commitment on an idea, entity, or cause without sufficient reflection. This commitment is too often a substitute for personal success or satisfaction. Referring to the fanatic or "true believer," Eric Hoffer writes:

> When our individual interests and prospects do not seem worth living for, we are in desperate need of something apart from us to live for. All forms of dedication, devotion, loyalty, and self-surrender are in essence a desperate clinging to something which might give worth and meaning to our futile, spoiled lives.[9]

Hoffer's description of fanatics and what sustains them is convincing, but not all forms of dedication and self-surrender qualify as fanatical. People can be thoughtfully dedicated to an ideal or a cause. Usually we can talk to these people and win their agreement to some of our points. Some conscientious religious groups even insist that their converts or applicants for positions of some power must challenge their cherished beliefs and think carefully on the commitment they are about to make. We must demur on the claim that all forms of dedication represent "a desperate clinging" to something that provides meaning to those making the commitment. However, there are fanatics, and an examination of their psychology can be useful in exploring how it is that war so often provides meaning in our lives.

Perhaps more important for present purposes is some attention to what might be called *fanaticism-lite* – the occurrence of occasional ill-considered enthusiasms in crowds or an individual's obsessive interest in a cause that interests relatively few. In the first category, excited enthusiasm may affect a large group of football fans or, more significantly, it may sweep over an entire nation in time of war. In the second category, a person may be obsessed with health foods and supplements. Herb (let us call him) may rave about the value of anti-oxidants and various minerals to every available captive audience, and he may devote many hours to spreading the word on his dietary beliefs. Or Lillian (let us call her) may try to convert everyone she meets to a particular view of Christianity. Neither of these persons is likely to be considered dangerous, because they do not have sufficient numbers to coerce others of us, and there are few social/cultural practices to encourage them. However, their psychological makeup may be similar to that of war lovers and political fanatics, so it is worth exploring.

What is it that drives Herb, the health foods and supplements devotee? His interest may be very like the interest another person has in history or science. A consuming interest is often the mark of highly intelligent, creative people. The mathematician Gauss, for example, was said to be frequently "seized by mathematics" and would fall silent, thinking about a mathematical problem, in the middle of a conversation. Such concentration may interfere with one's social relationships, but it is probably not a precursor to violence; it is not dangerous.

If, however, Herb is driven by an as yet unfulfilled desire for recognition and sees his advocacy of health foods as a way to obtain it, or if he has longed to feel part of some group and finds acceptance only with other health foods advocates, he may be a candidate for recruitment to a more troubling cause. The drive for recognition, for some form of personal success, is identified by Hoffer as characteristic of the fanatic. The desire to belong, to be recognized, is natural, but when the desire is not met, it may become an unconscious ultimate concern. Somehow it must be satisfied if life is to have meaning.

Similarly Lillian, who wishes to convert everyone to her brand of Christianity, may be driven by concern for her fellows, whose souls she believes are at risk. But if her conversion attempts are driven, like Herb's, by a desperate search for meaning, she too may be manipulated by a group whose cause is morally questionable.

Perhaps the most innocent of mild fanaticisms is the noisy enthusiasm of sports fans. The most dangerous element in this activity is the thoughtless contagion of enthusiasm that sometimes leads to stampedes and other forms of physical harm. There is danger, too, as Martha Nussbaum pointed out, that people will fail to recognize the emotional power of crowd contagion and, lacking such understanding, will easily submit to the expression of crowds in far more dangerous situations. Most people, however, leave exciting sport competitions and easily go back to everyday life. Their chosen team's winning does not become an almost ultimate concern, and their enthusiasm as fans is not driven by a deep concern for personal success.

The search for meaning can be a continuous, active work of construction and evaluation, or it can be a largely unconscious drive to satisfy a poorly defined longing. In the first case, we exercise control over what we do; in the second, we give up control to outside forces or vaguely felt inner longings. Why do we give up control? Consider a fairly common experience. I may take a few minutes away from my day's work, which is lagging a bit. I turn on the TV, ostensibly to make sure that "the world is still there." As I do so, I am ashamed to admit that I am half-hoping for something exciting – even a calamity of sorts – that will justify shifting my attention from work to a spectacle that can't be resisted. I want to give up control over my own decisions for a while. If a spectacle appears, I may say that I simply had no choice; I had to watch. If no spectacle appears, I chide myself for even thinking along these lines, breathe a sigh of relief that the world is still there, and go back to work. The freedom so frighteningly extolled by existentialists is fragile indeed.

In far more serious cases, people who volunteer for military service are sometimes glad to yield control over their own lives. They must simply obey orders. Some even welcome the opportunity to kill when they believe that they are not morally responsible for the killing. They may be relieved to give up the daily need to make a living, mow the lawn, repair the car, or tend to a long list of everyday chores. Freedom and responsibility are tightly bound together. Give up freedom and you also escape responsibility.

The desire *to see*, to observe a spectacle, is not only an invitation to escape, it is also an urge to be part of dramatic events. We noted in the chapter on masculinity and the warrior that J. G. Gray identified a "delight in seeing" as one of the enduring appeals of war:

> Seeing sometimes absorbs us utterly.... The eye is lustful because it requires the novel, the unusual, the spectacular. It cannot satiate itself on the familiar, the routine, the everyday.[10]

The spectacle takes us away from our routines. For at least a time, we feel part of something big, colorful, exciting. It is perhaps understandable that civilians are often more enthusiastic during wartime than soldiers who have experienced battle. The soldiers know that war is often boring and dirty as well as terrifying and colorful. Even so, after some years, an old soldier like Oliver Wendell Holmes, Jr., could brush aside his earlier description of the pain, boredom, and death of war and declare that "its message was divine."[11] The stench disappears, but the spectacle remains in memory's eye.

In this brief exploration of the human search for meaning, we can see that several features of war make a possible contribution: We join something bigger than ourselves, feel part of a great spectacle, allow ourselves to be controlled by outside forces (Sartre would say that we simply act in bad faith), and escape from the trivial responsibilities of everyday life. For those who have experienced little personal success, war holds the attraction of participating in national success. We noted earlier that young people who have had little success in school are more likely than their successful peers to join the armed forces.

As we have seen, there are enormously powerful forces playing on our psychological longings when war is involved. There are no parades or rousing songs for health food crusaders like Herb, and unless Lillian becomes a popular evangelist, she will find few followers. But mighty agencies of government and religion add their clout to traditional views of masculinity to make war a sacred duty that gives lives meaning.

Questions about the meaning of life have long been central to a rich liberal arts curriculum, but relatively few people have had access to such education, and we stubbornly refuse to share it at the high school level for all students. Indeed, many of those who believe that religion has given a preordained meaning to human life object to studies that they believe tend to "liberalize." Schools should not tell students what to believe about life's meaning, but they should help them to understand what a variety of thinkers have said on the topic and encourage reflective exploration. I have argued similarly on the topic of happiness in schools.[12] It is not the job of educators to *make* students happy or to define happiness for them but to acquaint them with a variety of interesting, well-expressed views on the topic and offer opportunities for guided exploration. Similarly, we should present and discuss views on the meaning of life. Further, this can be done in every course we teach. Instead, we leave many students in a state of unconscious longing and allow others to be controlled entirely by religion and/ or family. Perhaps the most immovable obstacle to enlightened, non-dogmatic education is the widespread belief that religious institutions and family have the right to indoctrinate, coupled with the coordinate belief that the schools have no right to counter this indoctrination with nondogmatic information and discussion. Indeed, even our finest institutions of higher learning come under fire for "liberalizing" their students. I'll say more about what schools might reasonably do about this problem in the next chapter.

We should spend some time on the twin problems of boredom and escape that attract so many people to war. Why is everyday life so often felt as boring?

EVERYDAY LIFE

Simone Weil wrote:

> Nothing is so beautiful and wonderful ... as the good. No desert is so dreary, monotonous, and boring as evil. This is the truth about authentic good and evil. With fictional good and evil it is the other way round. Fictional good is boring and flat, while fictional evil is varied and intriguing, attractive, profound, and full of charm.[13]

Roughly the same thing can be said of happy, productive, everyday life and warfare. Everyday life in fiction is usually boring; war is exciting. But actual everyday life at its best is not boring, and real war often is. Yet the idea persists and is pervasive. At the end of *Candide*, Voltaire describes his characters – Candide, Cunegondo, Pangloss, Martin, Cacambo, and the old woman – as suffering

> a boredom so excessive that one day the old woman dared to say to them: "I should like to know which is worse, to be raped a hundred times by Negro pirates, to have a buttock cut off, to run the gauntlet among the Bulgarians, to be whipped and flogged in an *auto-da-fe*, to be dissected, to row in a galley, in short to endure all the miseries through which we have passed, or to remain here doing nothing?"[14]

Human beings apparently crave excitement, and war is often thought to be exciting. It has been noted, however, that real war, as contrasted with fictional war, is actually boring. In *The Singapore Grip*, a young officer wonders

> whether war was of interest to anyone but the commanders who were conducting it. Was it not, for the troops themselves, a matter of standing around for hours on end speechless with boredom, perhaps with now and then a moment of terror?[15]

But, after encountering the hard-working, prosperous Turk, Candide and his companions return to their small farm, and each finds suitable work there. Cultivating their garden becomes, if not thrilling, somewhat satisfying.

The natural world may supply spectacles to please the eye. For those of us living near the ocean, sunrise provides a spectacle, and the sea itself varies from lakelike calm to thunderous turbulence. Every day there is something of drama in the natural world – fog, thrashing wind, drenching rain, the call of Canada geese in flight. Similarly, living near the mountains, one may be bewitched by the appearance and disappearance of peaks in the clouds, by the encompassing stillness after snowfall, by the chatter of a multitude of birds at the feeder. If spectacle is lacking in everyday life, it may be because we have forgotten where and how to look.

In *The Professor's House*, Willa Cather writes of the professor's enchantment with Lake Michigan. He, too, is sometimes afflicted with everyday boredom and the press of routine duties. Then he looks to the lake:

> But the great fact in life, the always possible escape from dullness, was the lake. The sun rose out of it, the day began there; it was like an open door that nobody could shut. The land and all its dreariness could never close in on you. You had only to look at the lake, and you knew you would soon be free.[16]

Earlier I mentioned Isaiah Berlin's comments about the temptation to retreat to the inner citadel and, with Berlin and many others, I rejected this as a permanent way of dealing with the problems of the real social world. However, most of us need a place (inner or outer) to which we can retreat occasionally to refresh our spirit. The church, temple, or mosque provides such a place for many people. A lakeside cabin attracts many, and a hike in the hills draws quite a few. Gardens give many of us the quiet, sensory pleasure, and physical challenge we need. The house itself can be a center of refuge and restoration.

Possibly no one has written more eloquently about the house than Gaston Bachelard.[17] Exploring the house as both a "group of organic habits" and a shelter for the imagination, Bachelard examines cellars, attics, doors, corners, nooks, and roofs. Reading Bachelard, one feels justified in curling up in a comfortable corner to daydream. One thinks about the meaning of life: Should I open the door and walk out into the world? Should I close and bolt it and tell myself that I am safe? Should I leave it ajar and remain wary and expectant?

Some readers will snort in irritation at Bachelard's description of polishing furniture, thereby increasing "the object's human dignity."[18] Ha! He would not write so poetically about rubbing a table with fragrant wax if he were assigned to housework all day. Perhaps not. For too many years, the home was thought to be a haven for men from the trials of a cruel public world, but it came to be regarded as a prison of boredom for women. Reading Bachelard, we might reconsider and reconstruct the house as both a refuge and a shelter for dreamers. The meaning we construct there establishes a foundation for meaning in the larger world, and what we learn in that world gives new meaning to our life inside.

The house is not only a shelter; it is also a center of activity. Often it is a place where we reconstruct our childhood or build the one we wish we'd had. The narrator in Wallace Stegner's *Angle of Repose* comments:

> When frontier historians theorize about the uprooted, the lawless, the purseless, and the socially cut-off who settled the West, they are not talking about people like my grandmother. So much that was cherished and loved, women like her had to give up; and the more they gave it up, the more they carried it helplessly with them.... For that sort of pioneer, the West was not a new country being created, but an old one being reproduced....[19]

Obviously in sympathy with his grandmother and many others who have found genuine meaning, not boredom, in everyday life, he continues by noting that space explorers and other electronic moderns are real, but sorry, pioneers:

> Their circuitry seems to include no atavistic domestic sentiment, they have suffered empathectomy, their computers hum no ghostly feedback of Home, Sweet Home. How marvelously free they are! How unutterably deprived![20]

For some of us, stories of the sort I've just discussed sustain us in our love of home and place. For others, all this is just piffle – the sort of piffle that kept women trapped at home. But there is more to the story of homes than houses and the reproduction of ways of life – lovely as that story is. Homes are centers for relation-building. Homes shelter not only individual dreamers but whole families. Elise Boulding describes the family as a small society:

> Here is an entity that has met catastrophe after catastrophe over many thousands of years, including the social catastrophes of the rise and fall of civilizations, with a unique combination of inventiveness, courage, and caring.[21]

For Boulding, family is not defined by traditional conventional groupings. Rather, it is "any household grouping which involves adults and children in continuing commitment to each other over time."[22] Boulding recognizes that not all families are happy; not all of them know how to resolve inevitable conflicts peaceably. But we can learn something about peacemaking and peaceable living from studying the best family groupings and how they influence the communities in which they dwell. As we saw earlier, Sara Ruddick has argued along a similar line.

We need not agree with Boulding on every detail or adopt the way she speaks of Quakerism, Taoism, and love of God. But the notion of the family as a small society is important. That small society, functioning well, is a source of meaning for all of its members. We cannot create the larger society in the precise image of the family; that is, we cannot simply "scale up," as policymakers are so fond of saying these days. What we can do is to get a deeper understanding of how people create or inculcate, sustain, or destroy meaning. In doing so, we will also acquire a deeper understanding of why people are torn between loving and hating war.

When people are bored, unsuccessful in their occupational life, unsatisfied in their social relationships, in need of change, or desperately seeking meaning, war may be an attractive means of escape. An unsatisfactory family life may induce the anxiety of meaninglessness discussed by Tillich, and its unhappy members may welcome the sense of purpose provided by military life and war.

But a strong, healthy family life does not guarantee that its members will shun war. On the contrary, they may feel morally and emotionally obligated to protect the family they love. If there is a strong tradition of military service, if masculinity is defined in terms of the warrior's courage (as it was in Theodore Roosevelt's family), children growing up in that family may embrace the warrior's role with pride.

For both war lovers and war haters, the destruction of a home-place may cause permanent trauma. The actual home and, by exten-sion, the nation-home are centers of meaning, and when they are threatened or destroyed, those suffering the loss may never recover. W. G. Sebald describes the reactions of Jean Amery, who suffered torture by the Nazis:

> The destruction of someone's native land is as one with that person's destruction.... "Home is the land of one's childhood and youth. Whoever has lost it remains lost himself, even if he has learned not to stumble about in the foreign country as if he were drunk."[23]

The dread of losing one's original source of meaning should make us hate war and violence passionately. But, paradoxically, when we are threatened with that loss, we may embrace war as the courageous way to prevent it.

# 10

## The Challenge to Education

Genuine education is aimed not merely at skills and a collection of facts – what Whitehead called "inert ideas" – but at a way of life that pursues understanding and an attitude of openness to new ideas and knowledge.[1] This aim is acknowledged today by a verbal emphasis on critical thinking, but not much attention is given to what is meant by critical thinking or what might be done to advance it. Too often it means presenting students with an argument about which they are indifferent and asking them to evaluate it on the basis of logical consistency, evidence offered and substantiated, and clarity of presentation. This is a useful exercise, but it is not adequate for our purposes here. We have been talking about loving and hating war, and that means that the arguments to be considered arise in a strong emotional climate.

In such a climate, a question arises immediately about whether, while acknowledging our own feelings, we can listen to possibly opposing views without prejudging them. Cass Sunstein has pointed out that we are afflicted by something he has called "group polarization"; we tend to believe those with whom we somehow identify and disbelieve or distrust those who belong to a different group.[2] One would think that in centers of higher learning such as universities this tendency would appear less often than in the general public. But many of us can – from decades of university experience – testify that this is not true. University audiences, like all others, have an ear keenly tuned to where a speaker is "coming from." If his or her social/political/theoretical identification is compatible with that of the listener, his or her remarks get considerable approval a priori. If not, listeners are busy concocting counterarguments before the speaker has even articulated his or her thoughts.

This attitude – to leap immediately to critical opposition – is so common that it is often defended as basic to critical thinking itself, but this is a mistake. I have frequently advised students to start their study by "reading and believing" without trying to pick apart and mount objections. What! Students are astonished and respond by telling me that this advice is contrary to their rigorous training in critical thinking. But when we undertake to read, say, Dewey or Piaget, we must read quite a lot before we are able to criticize intelligently. So, my advice stands: read, absorb, believe. Open-minded provisional belief is a tremendous aid to learning, and the belief involved is neither naive nor necessarily permanent. It is a strategic way of listening. Eventually, something the writer has written will challenge you, the reader, and you will have to put the bit of challenged text in the context of the whole work and explore what it is that seems wrong or inadequate.

If we want to think clearly about difficult matters, we do not start out by identifying the speaker as a republican, pragmatist, Catholic, or Iranian who *must* therefore be wrong. Instead, we listen. We may even come to shun labels. This does not imply that we must avoid all identification or refuse to stand united with a group whose main goal is one to which we are committed. But even in a spirit of solidarity, we should not accept an argument simply because it is "one of us" speaking. Further, we should occasionally question our affiliations and group identities. Why am I part of this group? What are the basic values to which we are committed? Are they internally consistent? Is our conduct consonant with these values?

One of our tasks as teachers is to present students with verifiable facts, and that is certainly part of what we should do in teaching about war. American students should be aware, for example, that the United States has used military force extensively throughout its entire history, and since 1950 has used military intervention dozens of times.[3] Today the United States spends as much on its military as the rest of the world combined. Students should also learn that in wars after 1940, civilian casualties have far outnumbered military casualties. They should know, too, that the United States maintains more than 700 military bases in thirty-nine other countries.

But how should these facts be presented? If they appear separately, as I have presented them here, or embedded in chronological discourse, they will become items in a set of inert facts soon to be forgotten. Realistically, to contribute to some understanding of war and peace, they have to be presented as part of a focused theme such as *militarism, American exceptionalism,* or *policing the world.* It is highly unlikely that units of study with such titles will be allowed. Perhaps we would be wise to use different titles, such as *serving our country, a light to the world,* or *protecting the world.* At least, thinking of such alternatives should remind us that there is more than one story to be told, and the underlying stories will have some influence on the way in which the facts are discussed. The question is whether those passionately committed to one story will allow the other to be presented at all. This is perhaps our greatest task in peace education – teaching people to listen to one another and maintain the lines of communication.

## PEACE EDUCATION

In the chapter on pacifism, I noted that there is a surprisingly large volume of literature on peace education. However, not much of it appears in the standard school curriculum, and we are left to wonder where it would fit. Now and then, a course or unit appears on conflict resolution, and once in a while a whole school is devoted to living and learning together in peace.[4] Among the numerous organizations and publications, there are several committed to research on peace and peace education.[5] Typically, however, the material presented in schools is devoted to peace in schools, to social justice and conflict resolution in schools. This is important work, but it does not go far enough; it does little to help students understand the love–hate relationship people maintain with war and the forces that manipulate their attitudes.

What follows is not a comprehensive review of peace education literature, nor is it a criticism of that literature. As we move along in the discussion of the challenges facing schools, it will become obvious that the forces supporting war are incredibly strong in the restraints they put upon efforts at peace education. Because the public school curriculum comes under public scrutiny so often and because there is unceasing criticism of efforts to "liberalize" our students, much valuable work on peace education takes place in religious institutions, colleges, and community forums. The tone in most of this work is understandably conciliatory, and in schools it is drastically limited.

The discussion of religion, for example, usually emphasizes the positive role religion plays in promoting peace. In one useful book on peace education, the authors recognize that "the great religions have contributed as much to war as to peace,"[6] but after that admission, the rest of the chapter is devoted to the concept of peace in various religions and the contributions they have made to both peace as the cessation of war and peace in the positive sense of social justice.

There is rarely any attempt to integrate the material in a way that forcefully illustrates the love–hate relationship we have discussed in this book. For example, in the peace education book mentioned above, it is acknowledged that John Dewey gave way in opposing U.S. participation in World War I and publicly supported it, but there is no discussion of the variety of pressures on Dewey and other academics to provide such support. Nor is there mention of how, in contrast, Jane Addams bravely and consistently stood up against the war. And there is no mention of Jeannette Rankin, the first woman elected to Congress, and her courageous vote against the war. Both Addams and Rankin suffered public disapproval as a result of their stands.

A general problem in the usual discussions of peace education is that the pain, obstacles, and struggles are often omitted or deemphasized. In the otherwise admirable book discussed above, for example, the work of Miles Horton and the Highlander School in educating for social justice is mentioned, but nothing is said about the resistance – sometimes violent – that Highlander's people experienced.[7] Students should be asked to consider: If your group is faced with public contempt, obstruction, and even death, do you persist in the struggle for social justice? Do you stand by your commitment to nonviolence? How?

Educators engaged in teaching for social justice face problems similar to those in peace education. They must find exactly the right language in which to present their material or risk being labeled "unpatriotic," "socialist," "anti-capitalist," or "radical."[8] Even with great care, it may be impossible to discuss how religions have contributed to war unless we confine our discussion to events long past. In exploring the Catholic Church's role in social justice, consider how difficult it is to discuss liberation theology fairly.

If we are serious about educating for an understanding of peace and war, we must consider new approaches. Although we can learn much from past educational efforts, there really isn't much in earlier American education to help us with the problems we have addressed here. In an otherwise informative (and highly critical) discussion of education and war, Christopher Leahey asks how we can encourage our students to think critically about America's wars. He writes:

> My answer to this question is simple: let's set aside standards-based learning initiatives, compromised textbooks, and high-stakes exams, and return to our democratic tradition of education that views learning as a continual process where students actively engage in authentic inquiry, exploring the past, and constructing knowledge.[9]

But there has been no such democratic tradition in our public schools. Despite the efforts of strong reformers such as Rugg and Dewey in the past, the American curriculum has continued to emphasize nationalistic patriotism, American exceptionalism, and the positive role of American power in the world. Moreover, it is not simply a matter of revising the history curriculum. The great aims of education, including educating for peace, must be thoughtfully embedded in the entire curriculum.

To do this and to meet the needs of twenty-first-century living, we should rethink the discipline-oriented structure of our schools. The major changes required will not be accomplished overnight. The disciplines, carefully separated from one another and, too often, separated also from real life, have been basic to schooling for centuries. But we can start by stretching the disciplines from within.[10] The sharp separation of disciplines has not served us well, but because it is so entrenched, our response to new aims or subjects has been, and still is, to "add a course." The resulting curriculum is thus crowded with courses that compete for time. In the social studies, where we would expect to find most of the material addressing peace education, the competition among politics, economics, sociology, anthropology, geography, civics, and even psychology has been dominated by the continuing competition of history against all the rest. The most promising solution to this disciplinary schizophrenia is the issue orientation to social studies promoted by Harold Rugg in the 1920s, 1930s, and early 1940s. Rugg claimed, rightly I think, that sharply divided disciplines impede education for understanding:

> Nothing short of genius on the part of a student could create an ordered understanding of modern life from such a compartmentalized arrangement of material.[11]

But Rugg's textbooks were branded un-American and subversive, and they disappeared from the public schools.

To teach effectively toward the major aims of education, we must address those aims in every course we teach. The aims should guide the selection of material throughout the curriculum and provide unity and integrity. It would be better, as mentioned earlier, if we could discard the ancient curriculum organized around discrete disciplines, but that is unlikely to happen in the near future. Therefore, we must ask how each of the subjects in the current curriculum can contribute to the aim of understanding war and peace. In earlier chapters, I gave examples of what we might do in teaching for an understanding of war and peace. Now I want to add a bit to those ideas. In the suggestions that follow, I concentrate on the secondary curriculum.

Literature is a natural and powerful partner in the study of history, and its use in peace education should be increased. The literature on World War I provides a useful example. Earlier in this book I mentioned *All Quiet on the Western Front, Birdsong, Goodbye to All That, Three Guineas*, and the poetry of that war. The conflict in attitudes toward war found in the poetry of Rupert Brooke and Wilfred Owen is worth considerable attention. Brooke's loving – almost romantic – attachment to England, regardless of the suffering required to defend it, contrasts sharply with Owen's disgust and revulsion toward the blood and horror of the war. Giving attention to both should help to make possible a full and fair discussion of patriotism and war. If teachers add to this a discussion of Yeats's treatment of Owen's poetry, students may get some sense of the love–hate relationship that has so long characterized the human attitude toward war.

Lyn Macdonald, editor of *Anthem for Doomed Youth*, in which the previously mentioned poetry appears, remarks at the end of her Introduction to the volume, "It is sad to think that the poetry of the First World War has become political and the touchstone by which people are tempted to form judgements."[12] Many of us do not think it is sad that this poetry has inspired political debate and judgment over war. We do not wish to confine poetry to a narrow disciplinary niche. That difference of opinion, too, is worth further exploration.

Should literature be chosen for its relevance to the aims of peace education or to any aims other than the appreciation of literature? The answer implied and now stated outright in this book is *yes, of course*. Everything we do in schools should be guided by, or at least compatible with, our major aims. The literature chosen for this purpose should be of high quality; it should not be mere propaganda; and it should invite thought, even a measure of consternation. Fine literature that addresses controversial issues may evoke a temporary reaction – "I don't know what to think!" – that will lead to further investigation. Starting the selection of literature with themes rather than the names of writers can help us break down the suffocating barriers of demarcation erected by the disciplines.

It also makes sense to choose literature that has had continuing influence on the themes in question. The *Iliad*, for example, has been prized as great literature, but it has also been referred to repeatedly in discussions of masculinity and the depravity induced by battle. I mentioned earlier Simone Weil's essay "The Poem of Force" and Jonathan Shay's recent account of soldiers going berserk in battle, *Achilles in Vietnam*. When the *Iliad* is chosen for both its literary quality and its lessons for peace and war, teachers must remember not to get bogged down in the names of characters, the use of metaphor, and the technicalities of literary composition. The main point is to think deeply about the human inclination to kill and destroy, and what it does to both those who are its victims and those who give way to it and become perpetrators.

How can classes in mathematics serve the aim of understanding peace and war? Most obviously, time can be spent on adding things up: the cost of war, the cost of maintaining a huge military, the cost of rebuilding cities destroyed. Students might consult President Dwight Eisenhower's early speech on the sacrifices made by deciding to commit huge amounts of money to the military.[13] How many schools could be built for the price of one heavy bomber? How many new homes could be built for the price of a single destroyer? Eisenhower spoke specifically and cogently on these questions.

Students could also gather and discuss casualty figures. How have they changed over centuries of warfare? Why have modern wars claimed so many civilian lives? Can the deliberate targeting of civilians be morally justified? This discussion should not be confined to mere numbers; it should include at least a few stories, and students should become familiar with the names of places: Hamburg, London, Dresden, Pearl Harbor, Tokyo, Hiroshima, Nagasaki. There should also be some discussion of competing ethical theories. Could firebombing and nuclear bombing of cities be defended under Kantianism? How about Utilitarianism?

Now the objection may be raised that mathematics teachers are not prepared to discuss ethical theories and war narratives; if this is true, and I fear that it is, the only reasonable response is to say that, if we are serious in our pursuit of large educational aims, *they should be so prepared.* Mathematics is part, and should be an integral part, of an education aimed at understanding and wisdom. What is the point of teaching everyone to factor trinomials and graph linear equations if most people will never have a need for such skills? Students may be motivated to study mathematics, however, if they can see some connection to the larger problems of human existence. Consider, too, the oddity of forcing high school students to study five or more subjects to ensure a "well-rounded" education when they are taught by people who know only one subject. I do not suggest that teachers should be equally conversant in all subjects. Rather, I suggest that they should be well-educated generalists first and specialists second. Possibly the best way to prepare such teachers is to structure the study of their major subject in a way that emphasizes its history and its connection to other subjects and human interests.

Attention to biographical accounts should enhance both the study of mathematics and its relevance to broader aims. The case of Bertrand Russell is instructive for present purposes. A prominent mathematician and philosopher, Russell strongly opposed Britain's participation in World War I. He took a position very like the one that we've been discussing throughout this book – that the abolition of war will require important changes in human psychology in addition to economic and political changes. On our faulty psychology and the behavior of citizens during the lead-up to war, he wrote:

> The attitude of ordinary men and women during the first months amazed me, particularly the fact that they found a kind of pleasure in the excitement.[14]

This pleasure in excitement is revealed again and again:

> [M]ost of us still prefer passion to intelligence, we like to admire and we like to hate, we like to see things in black and white. Our whole mental apparatus is that which is appropriate to sending us rushing into battle with hoarse war-cries.[15]

Russell was also outspoken on the traditional conceptions of masculinity and femininity. Like Woolf, who found both ideas hateful, Russell heaps scorn on the "he-man" and adds, "Correlative to the he-man is the she-woman, who is equally undesirable."[16] They (the he-man and the she-woman) support and encourage each other in ways that sustain warlike attitudes, and Russell comments further, "So the more they love each other, the worse they both become."[17] Arguing for the exercise of intelligence, Russell challenges the man–woman relationship prescribed by the Bible, placing it in the context of force and submission:

> The only basis for this view was that if wives could be induced to accept it, it saved trouble for their husbands. "The man is not of the woman but the woman of the man; neither was the man created for the woman, but the woman for the man" (1 Corinthians xi, 8, 9). I defy anyone to find any basis for this view, except that men have stronger muscles than women.[18]

Here we see Russell exercising some humor as well as scorn. Some people, of course, would point to the biblical story of Adam and Eve as the basis for the view he rejects, and Russell would again be astonished and dismayed. *Read* it, he might counsel, *think!* Surely you don't believe that! In the spirit I am advocating, we should not believe things simply because so-and-so said them or because they appeared in a book (even the Bible), but neither should we discard them without further thought. Many of our most powerful myths are literally false, yet worthy of deeper thought. How can we understand the Adamic myth? Paul Ricoeur answers, "In the first place, it means accepting the fact that it is a myth."[19] Then perhaps we can move on intelligently from there.

Russell is sometimes too scornful, too hasty in branding ideas and expressions as products of intelligence or passion – too black and white – despite his own criticism of that attitude. However, he is also an engaging writer with a delightful sense of humor. Students may be fascinated to hear (in math class!) that Russell (a mathematician!) received the Nobel Prize in literature in 1950.

In the chapter on patriotism, we noted that patriotic songs, parades, and martial music are important features of national celebration. Such music is used to create solidarity. Recall Dexter Filkins mentioning how he watched young marines, expert killers, singing together. In churches, hymn singing by the congregation is designed not only to worship God but also to unite the singers as one body.

In music class, those hoarse war cries mentioned by Russell might be explored further. They have a fearsome history. Screaming at the enemy while attacking strikes fear into the enemy and bolsters the courage of the attackers, perhaps by distracting them from their own vulnerability. Martial music has been used for dual purposes – to scare the wits out of the enemy and to assure the attacking soldiers that they are synchronized in their efforts. The bagpipes and drums of the Scots sent chills through their enemies, bugles on the western frontier announced the arrival of the cavalry, and wild war cries have terrorized those about to be attacked throughout history.[20] On the home front and in military training, killing chants increase hatred and the desire to fight.

Music class should not be turned into a session of amateur psychoanalysis. Students should not be required to report how they feel as they listen to various kinds of music, but they should be allowed to do so if they wish. The point is to help students understand how cultures have used music to encourage love, hate, solidarity, enmity, action, and ease. Listen to "The Star-Spangled Banner" and then to Brahms's "Lullaby." What feelings are induced? Would anyone use a Sousa march to rock a baby to sleep? Can we imagine an army marching to "As Time Goes By" or "Close to You"? Why do we associate most peace music – "Where Have All the Flowers Gone?" or "Whatever Happened to Peace on Earth?" – with a counterculture? Daniel Levitin asks:

> Why does music have such power to move us? Pete Seeger says it is because of the way that medium and meaning combine in song, the combination of form and structure uniting with an emotional message.[21]

Some music pushes us to dance or at least tap our feet, some into sentimental memories, some into an expansion of soul, some into slumber. Marching music gets us moving together; it is a great synchronizer. Music teachers and physical education (PE) teachers could profitably work together to help students understand the power of marching music.

What else might be done in PE classes to further the aim of peace education? Once again, we have to avoid the temptation to add a class.

This is what sometimes happened when PE teachers were asked to do something about health and nutrition. But we don't have to add a class; we simply have to stretch the curriculum from within. Teachers should invite students to talk about the connection between sports and warfare. The emotional excitement mentioned by Russell in reaction to war is a regular, expected response to competition in sports. Free analytic discussion can help students to understand and control their own responses to sporting events. They should also learn that the connection between vigorous competition in sports and a fighting spirit in war has long been recognized. They should hear and discuss the Duke of Wellington's famous remark that Great Britain's battles in the Napoleonic wars were won on the playing fields of Eton. Should this make us more dedicated to preparing young men for war or more determined to sever the connection between sports and war?

Anyone who has taught at the secondary level knows that there is some tension between faculty members who teach academic courses and those who teach vocational courses and PE. PE teachers are often resented for taking up time and resources that would be better spent on courses that aim at intellectual growth. It is especially odd that teachers well grounded in classical history should take this attitude. Have they forgotten the Greek insistence on the interdependence of sound minds and sound bodies? More likely, the resentment is part of the affliction we are addressing – the narrow compartmentalization of subject matter that characterizes contemporary education. It should not seem odd to expect PE teachers to read, explore, and discuss issues that are an integral part of genuine education.

The visual arts, too, have something important to contribute to peace education. Virginia Woolf hoped that the vivid photography available from the Spanish Civil War and World War I might so sicken viewers that they would reject war entirely. Alluding to Woolf's hope, Susan Sontag writes:

> Not to be pained by these pictures, not to recoil from them, not to strive to abolish what causes this havoc, this carnage – these for Woolf would be the reactions of a moral monster. And … we are not monsters. … Our failure is one of imagination, of empathy; we have failed to hold this reality in mind.[22]

Sontag follows this by noting that identity – national or religious – tends to overwhelm our sympathy for human beings in general. We discussed this in Chapter 4 in connection with the emotional force of nationalism in contrast to the thinness of cosmopolitanism. When pictures show our own people suffering as victims, we are horrified, but we also become angry. Pictures, like stories or music, can induce hatred as well as sympathy and love.

For some years, we thought that art and music appreciation courses might increase sympathy for and understanding of other cultures. Those courses have disappeared from the curricula of many American schools, but perhaps their greatest effect was merely to separate an "educated" class from one less educated. It was a mark of being educated to be familiar with the names Beethoven, Brahms, Titian, Michelangelo, and Picasso. But, as we have seen, this educated class has been no more resistant to war than those less privileged.

In Chapter 2, in a discussion of war and destruction, I quoted Jonathan Glover on the fatal combination of technology and the destructive side of human psychology.[23] I believe he is right. Massive technology has been developed to carry out widespread destruction of life and property. And, of course, there are collaborative groups in business and politics. We educators can do little about these forces, but we can do something about the psychology.

All educators must become keenly aware of their responsibility to promote moral awareness and a commitment to peace. I have given just a few examples of how teachers of literature, mathematics, music, PE, and art might participate in this effort. Now we must consider science.

As a school subject, science – like the other subjects – is already damaged by severe compartmentalization. It must change to meet the challenges we have been discussing. E. O. Wilson predicts that this will happen: that scientists will connect with one another across the epistemological divide that has separated the academic disciplines. Indeed, he suggests that this *must* happen:

> There is, in my opinion, an inevitability to the unity of knowledge. It reflects real life. The trajectory of world events suggests that educated people should be far better able than before to address the great issues courageously and analytically by undertaking a traverse of disciplines.[24]

In this brief discussion of how we might stretch science education to address problems of peace education, I'll concentrate on just one area that needs immediate and dedicated attention: the separation of intellectual science from morality. We are all familiar with horrific stories of scientific immorality: Nazi doctors performing criminal operations on Jews, American scientists withholding treatment from prisoners at Tuskegee, forced sterilization of people thought to be mentally incompetent, the centuries'-long brutal treatment of the mentally ill. Most of these well-known cases involve clear cases of moral wrong.

There are other, more complex and ambiguous, cases. Should scientists and physicians be involved in work that will cause harm or death to large numbers of people? Scientists working on the development of the atomic bomb suffered various levels of moral doubt. Some – for example, Leo Szilard – expressed moral concern before the first bomb was dropped; he advised against using it. Others – Robert Oppenheimer, for example – expressed concern afterward, fearing for the future of the world. Scientific work done during war – the work done by, for example, James Conant – poses a moral dilemma: The use of certain weapons is immoral, but neglecting to develop them may place one's own country in jeopardy if they are developed and used by the enemy. Acknowledging the dilemma, we can still ask whether the development of poison gases, agent orange, and other chemical weapons can ever be justified.

These are matters that high school students should think about. Recently, I heard the account of a related classroom experience. A biology class was finishing a unit on the effects of tobacco on human health. The teacher, who knew that several of her students had planned careers in commercial art, asked her class how they would respond to an offer of a commission to provide artwork for a tobacco advertisement. A male student replied immediately: "No, I couldn't do that ... well, probably I wouldn't. But if I had no other offers ... well, I hope I wouldn't. I don't know." This teacher's class was led to think honestly about the tensions between economic self and moral self and, by extension, between the welfare of one's own nation and that of others. That is probably all we can do as educators. In handling highly controversial issues, we cannot – usually should not – tell our students what they should believe and act upon, but we can get them to think.

### BALANCING FACTS AND MEMORIES

Thoughtful educators and historians in the United States often complain that the history taught in our schools fails to address the morally questionable side of America's history: exceptionalism; militarism; unnecessary destruction; racial, ethnic, and gender bias; failure to provide opportunities to critique religion; bias in the presentation of material on class differences. Critical theorists have been outspoken on these issues, but their efforts have had little effect on the development of textbooks.

We need to find intelligent ways to address these issues. When we want to include a unit on American militarism, for example, I suggest that we might find a more acceptable title for it. This is not meant to disguise or set aside the issue but to make it possible to include it at all. Then we must be sure that the treatment is fair, recognizing the great pride many citizens take in the military and its history.

Gordon Wood has recently described the problem faced by historians. Discussing the work of Bernard Bailyn, Wood writes: "Critical history-writing is all head and no heart."[25] The relentless search for facts, stripped of feelings, does not do justice to what people have actually experienced, and the choice of facts is itself unavoidably colored by unspoken feelings. Further, the memory of events is loaded with controversy. It is hard to say unarguably, "Here's how it was," when others standing beside us say, "That's not the way I saw it." Wood comments:

> While memory may be shaped and informed by critical history, history "may be kept alive, made vivid and constantly relevant and urgent by the living memory we have of it." Memory is as important to our society as the history written by academics.[26]

What this means for a project in peace education that, admittedly, is closer to the critical theorists than to traditionalists is the recognition of what might be called the *memory of memories*. Educators must be careful not to treat loved memories – even when they are demonstrably wrong – with scorn. Instead, we have to shape those memories gently, neither passing them along without criticism nor trying to abolish them entirely. Instead of refusing to participate in patriotic rituals and celebrations, as Virginia Woolf suggested – and I have great respect for her suggestion – we might try to modify them. Veterans might be honored not by parades and reenactments of battles but by services that emphasize our mourning. Solemn remembrance and regret would be central to such occasions. No rifles or cannon would be shot off.

Educators and policymakers sometimes think, as some critical historians do, that the solution to emotional clashes of memory is to eliminate any reference to the feelings involved. This is the solution ultimately decided upon by authorities at the Smithsonian Museum with respect to the exhibition of the *Enola Gay*, planned to commemorate the bombing of Hiroshima fifty years earlier. Debate over what should be said about the *Enola Gay's* mission was so heated that, eventually, only the plane itself and a few words about its development and the bomb it dropped appeared in an emotionally and ethically sterile exhibit. Recounting the story of this fierce debate and its outcome, Michael Bess asks:

> What should we remember about our past, and what should we allow to fade into oblivion? In what kind of light should our nation's past deeds be portrayed? Who decides, and how? What does it mean to have a constructive and honest relationship with our past?[27]

An honest and constructive relationship with topics on peace and war requires attention to both feelings and facts. We should address not only what happened but also how people feel about the events under discussion and, where possible, why they feel as they do. It is in the last part of the discussion – *why* we feel as we do – that critical theory might help to clear up the facts.

Efforts to reduce attention to feelings and opinions have often arisen in intellectual life. As early as the seventeenth century, there was a movement to eliminate figurative language from clerical writing. The idea, David Noble writes, was to employ

> "languages containing only words which were direct reflections of concrete reality, and nothing else." … In 1670, Samuel Parker, bishop of Oxford and president of Magdalen College, Oxford, went so far as to introduce a bill in Parliament "to fine all divines caught using metaphors."[28]

We are all familiar with Dickens's Thomas Gradgrind, who wanted children to be taught only the Facts and never to wonder.[29] Indeed, poetry and poetic language were regarded with suspicion from the time of Plato, who, despite his concern about the bad influence of poetry, was himself a master of metaphor. Similarly, fiction was forbidden by some schoolmasters and clerics well into the twentieth century. Analytic philosophers, too, thought it both possible and desirable to remove opinion from the analysis of language, insisting on strict and unambiguous denotation and verifiable predication.

We know better now. Human beings are emotional creatures. Miguel Unamuno put it this way:

> Man is said to be a reasoning animal. I do not know why he has not been defined as an affective or feeling animal. Perhaps that which differentiates him from other animals is feeling rather than reason. More often have I seen a cat reason than laugh or weep. Perhaps it weeps or laughs inwardly – but then perhaps, also inwardly, the crab resolves equations of the second degree.[30]

We are moved by music, spectacles, words, collective sighs and motions, and religious exhortations; we feel love, hatred, fear, loneliness, joy, anger, and anxiety. We know also that many nonhuman animals both think and feel. That knowledge should help to reduce human arrogance.

It might rightly be said that genuine education begins with feeling (the twinge we call *interest*) and moves toward wisdom as we think openly and clearly about what we feel. To that end, schools must move beyond the weary, highly unrealistic organization of knowledge into narrowly defined disciplines and begin to address great universal aims such as happiness, existential meaning, what it means to be a moral person, and our role as individuals and members of various groups in promoting peace. The pursuit of any of these aims requires not only that we speak freely but also that we listen openly and lovingly.

In this book, I have not said much about the psychology of our leaders (other than Theodore Roosevelt), although that topic is worth exploring,[31] and I have not discussed the economic and political causes of war. Others more competent in these matters have written mountains of volumes on them. My concern has been focused on what educators can do to help our students and ourselves better understand what makes us love and hate war. Although I believe that most of my suggestions are both reasonable and theoretically feasible, I fear that they will not soon be employed in schools. The very things that stand in the way of their implementation also support the continuation of war.

# NOTES

## INTRODUCTION

1. See, for example, Nel Noddings, ed., *Educating Citizens for Global Awareness* (New York: Teachers College Press, 2005).
2. Simone Weil, "The *Iliad*, Poem of Might," in *Simone Weil Reader*, ed. George A. Panichas (Mt. Kisco, NY: Moyer Bell Ltd., 1977), pp. 153–183.
3. J. G. Gray, *The Warriors: Reflections on Men in Battle* (Lincoln: University of Nebraska Press, 1970), p. 29.
4. William James, *The Varieties of Religious Experience* (New York: Modern Library, 1929), p. 359.
5. On chastened patriotism, see Jean Bethke Elshtain, *Women and War* (New York: Basic Books, 1987).
6. Paul Tillich, *The Courage to Be* (New Haven, CT: Yale University Press, 1952).
7. Gaston Bachelard, *The Poetics of Space*, trans. Maria Jolas (New York: Orion Press, 1964), p. 6.

## 1. THE CENTRALITY OF WAR IN HISTORY

1. See Francis Fukuyama, *The End of History and the Last Man* (New York: Free Press, 1992).
2. Samuel P. Huntington, *The Clash of Civilizations and the Remaking of World Order* (New York: Simon & Schuster, 1996).
3. Robert Kagan, *The Return of History and the End of Dreams* (New York: Vintage Books, 2008).
4. On the stability of older democracies, see Jared Diamond, *Guns, Germs, and Steel* (New York: W. W. Norton, 2005).
5. Robert L. O'Connell, *Ride of the Second Horseman: The Birth and Death of War* (Oxford: Oxford University Press, 1995), p. 239.
6. See John Mueller, *Retreat from Doomsday: The Obsolescence of Major War* (New York: Basic Books, 1989).

7. Clark Wissler, *Indians of the United States* (New York: Anchor Books, 1989), p. 242.
8. See Richard Wrangham and Dale Peterson, *Demonic Males: Apes and the Origins of Human Violence* (New York: Houghton Mifflin, 1996).
9. See Regina M. Schwartz, *The Curse of Cain: The Violent Legacy of Monotheism* (Chicago: University of Chicago Press, 1997).
10. See Sara Ruddick, *Maternal Thinking: Toward a Politics of Peace* (Boston: Beacon Press, 1989).
11. Jean Bethke Elshtain and Sheila Tobias, eds., *Women, Militarism, and War* (Savage, MD: Rowman & Littlefield, 1990).
12. For a useful discussion of this problem, see Birgit Brock-Utne, *Educating for Peace: A Feminist Perspective* (New York and Oxford: Pergamon Press, 1985); see also Betty A. Reardon, *Sexism and the War System* (New York: Teachers College Press, 1985).
13. See James Dawes, *The Language of War* (Cambridge, MA: Harvard University Press, 2002).
14. Jacques Derrida, *Of Grammatology*, trans. Gayatri Chakravorty Spivak (Baltimore: Johns Hopkins University Press, 1976), p. 112. See also the discussion in Dawes, *Language of War*.
15. Ruddick, *Maternal Thinking*, p. 189.
16. Martin Buber, *I and Thou*, trans. Walter Kaufmann (New York: Charles Scribner's Sons, 1970), p. 56.
17. On who serves in the military, see Michael Massing, "The Volunteer Army: Who Fights and Why?" *New York Review of Books* 55 (April 3, 2008): 34–46.
18. Rudyard Kipling, "Tommy," in *Kipling: A Selection of His Stories and Poems*, vol.II, ed. John Beecroft (Garden City, NY: Doubleday, 1956), pp. 491–492.
19. Rupert Brooke, "The Soldier," in *Anthem for Doomed Youth*, ed. Lyn Macdonald (London: Folio Society, 2000), p. 18.
20. See Wilfred Owen, "Dulce et Decorum Est," in *Anthem for Doomed Youth*, p. 200.
21. James Tatum, *The Mourner's Song* (Chicago: University of Chicago Press, 2004), p. 20.
22. I discuss this in the chapter on war and violence in *The Maternal Factor: Two Paths to Morality* (Berkeley: University of California Press, 2010).
23. Dexter Filkins, *The Forever War* (New York: Alfred A. Knopf, 2008), ch. 18.
24. Michael Walzer, *Just and Unjust Wars* (New York: Basic Books, 1977), p. xiii.
25. Ibid., pp. 329–335. Martin Buber also made the point against Gandhi that nonviolence could not be effective against the immoral violence of the Nazis. See Buber, *Pointing the Way*, trans. and ed. Maurice Friedman (New York: Harper & Row, 1957), pp. 139–147.
26. Walzer, *Just and Unjust Wars*, p. 335.

27. Jeff McMahan, *Killing in War* (Oxford: Clarendon Press, 2009).
28. Quoted in Michael True, *An Energy Field More Intense Than War* (Syracuse, NY: Syracuse University Press, 1995), p. 81.
29. See many examples in Anthony Swofford, *Jarhead* (New York: Scribner, 2003); also see J. G. Gray, *The Warriors: Reflections on Men in Battle* (Lincoln: University of Nebraska Press, 1959 and 1970).
30. McMahan, *Killing in War*, pp. 128–130.
31. Ibid., p. 122.
32. See Lorrie Goldensohn, *Dismantling Glory* (New York: Columbia University Press, 2003); Gray, *The Warriors*; and Jonathan Shay, *Achilles in Vietnam: Combat Trauma and the Undoing of Character* (New York: Scribner, 1994).

## 2. DESTRUCTION

1. Michael True, *An Energy Field More Intense Than War* (Syracuse, NY: Syracuse University Press, 1995), p. 81.
2. Dexter Filkins, *The Forever War* (New York: Alfred A. Knopf, 2008), pp. 116–117.
3. Jonathan Shay, *Achilles in Vietnam: Combat Trauma and the Undoing of Character* (New York: Scribner, 1994), p. 5.
4. Drew Gilpin Faust, *This Republic of Suffering: Death and the American Civil War* (New York: Alfred A. Knopf, 2008), p. xi.
5. Ibid., p. 175.
6. Ibid., p. 38.
7. Quoted in J. G. Gray, *The Warriors: Reflections on Men in Battle* (Lincoln: Nebraska University Press, 1959 and 1970), p. 223. See also the account in Faust, *This Republic of Suffering*, p. 271, and in Louis Menand, *The Metaphysical Club* (New York: Farrar, Strauss and Giroux, 2001).
8. Lorrie Goldensohn, *Dismantling Glory* (New York: Columbia University Press, 2003), p. 73.
9. See Shay, *Achilles in Vietnam*.
10. Michael Bess, *Choices Under Fire: Moral Dimensions of World War II* (New York: Alfred A. Knopf, 2006), p. 110.
11. George Packer, "Embers," *The New Yorker*, February 1, 2010: 33.
12. See Geoffrey C. Ward and Ken Burns, *The War: An Intimate History 1941–1945* (New York: Alfred A. Knopf, 2007).
13. See Susan Sontag, "Looking at War," *The New Yorker*, December 9, 2002: 82–98; also Virginia Woolf, *Three Guineas* (New York: Harcourt Brace, 1938/1966).
14. W. G. Sebald, *On the Natural History of Destruction*, trans. Anthea Bell (New York: Random House, 2003), p. 25.
15. Ibid.
16. Jorg Friedrich, *The Fire: The Bombing of Germany 1940–1945* (New York: Columbia University Press, 2006), p. 166.

17. Ibid., p. 167.
18. Sebald, *Natural History of Destruction*, p. 30.
19. Quoted in Nicholson Baker, *Human Smoke: The Beginnings of World War II, the End of Civilization* (New York: Simon & Schuster, 2008), p. 152.
20. Friedrich, *The Fire*, p. 469.
21. Peter Schrijvers, *The GI War Against Japan* (New York: New York University Press, 2002), pp. 241–242.
22. Ibid., p. 248.
23. Ibid., p. 247.
24. Jonathan Glover, *Humanity: A Moral History of the 20th Century* (New Haven, CT: Yale University Press, 2000), p. 414.
25. Primo Levi, *The Drowned and the Saved*, trans. Raymond Rosenthal (New York: Vintage Books, 1988), p. 25.
26. Ibid. Amery's case is also mentioned by Glover, *Humanity*, and discussed at some length by Sebald, *Natural History of Destruction*.
27. Levi, *Drowned and the Saved*, p. 75.
28. Ibid., p. 76.
29. Gray, *Warriors*, p. 163.
30. Ibid., chapter 6.
31. Shay, *Achilles in Vietnam*, p. 33.
32. Ibid.
33. Ibid., especially chapter 1.
34. Testimony given for the Vietnam Veterans Against the War, quoted in Goldensohn, *Dismantling Glory*, pp. 255–256.
35. Ibid.
36. Ibid., p. 81.
37. Ibid., p. 41.

## 3. MASCULINITY AND THE WARRIOR

1. Evan Thomas, *The War Lovers: Roosevelt, Lodge, Hearst, and the Rush to Empire, 1898* (New York: Little, Brown, 2010), p. 43.
2. Richard Wrangham and Dale Peterson, *Demonic Males: Apes and the Origins of Human Violence* (New York: Houghton Mifflin, 1996), p. 23.
3. Ibid., p. 113.
4. Ibid., p. 115.
5. Ibid., p. 251.
6. See Lee Alan Dugatkin, *The Altruism Equation* (Princeton, NJ: Princeton University Press, 2006).
7. Ibid., p. 61.
8. Ibid., p. 65.
9. Jared Diamond, *Guns, Germs, and Steel* (New York: W. W. Norton, 2005), p. 281.
10. Ibid., p. 278.

11. Carl G. Jung, *Answer to Job*, in *Collected Works*, vol. 2 (Princeton, NJ: Princeton University Press, 1969), p. 395.

12. Ibid., pp. 447–448.

13. Jack Miles, *God: A Biography* (New York: Alfred A. Knopf, 1995), p. 294.

14. Ibid., p. 302.

15. See the articles in Susan Frank Parsons, ed., *The Cambridge Companion to Feminist Theology* (Cambridge: Cambridge University Press, 2002).

16. See, for example, Mary Daly, *Beyond God the Father* (Boston: Beacon Press, 1974); J. Anthony Phillips, *Eve: The History of an Idea* (San Francisco: Harper & Row, 1984); Nel Noddings, *Women and Evil* (Berkeley: University of California Press, 1989); Adrienne Rich, *Of Woman Born* (New York: W. W. Norton, 1976).

17. Nel Noddings, *The Maternal Factor: Two Paths to Morality* (Berkeley: University of California Press, 2010).

18. Susan Moller Okin, *Women in Western Political Thought* (Princeton, NJ: Princeton University Press, 1979), p. 306. The quoted passages are from Allan Bloom, "Interpretive Essay," in *The Republic of Plato*, trans. Bloom (New York: Basic Books, 1968), p. 380.

19. Okin, *Women in Western Political Thought*, pp. 87–88. The Aristotle quote is from *Eudemian Ethics*, VII, 1238b.

20. James Gilligan, *Violence* (New York: G. P. Putnam's Sons, 1996), p. 267.

21. Michael S. Kimmel, "Clarence, William, Iron Mike, Tailhook, Senator Packwood, Spur Posse, Magic … and Us," in *Transforming a Rape Culture*, ed. Emilie Buchwald, Pamela R. Fletcher, and Martha Roth (Minneapolis: Milkweed Editions, 1993), p. 123.

22. See, for example, Estella Lauter and Carol Schrier Rupprecht, eds., *Feminist Archetypal Theory* (Knoxville: University of Tennessee Press, 1985).

23. Lorrie Goldensohn, *Dismantling Glory* (New York: Columbia University Press, 2003), p. 331.

24. J. G. Gray, *The Warriors: Reflections on Men in Battle* (Lincoln: University of Nebraska Press, 1959/1970), pp. 28–29.

25. Ibid.

26. Seth L. Schein, *The Mortal Hero* (Berkeley: University of California Press, 1984), p. 84.

27. Ibid., p. 82.

28. Paul Tillich, *The Courage to Be* (New Haven, CT: Yale University Press, 1952), p. 5.

29. Simone Weil, "The Poem of Might," in *Simone Weil Reader*, ed. George A. Panichas (Mt. Kisco, NY: Moyer Bell Ltd., 1977), pp. 153–154.

30. Schein, *Mortal Hero*, p. 83.

31. Jonathan Shay, *Achilles in Vietnam: Combat Trauma and the Undoing of Character* (New York: Scribner, 1994), p. 77.

32. Dexter Filkins, *The Forever War* (New York: Alfred A. Knopf, 2008), p. 90.

160  *Notes to Pages 48–56*

33. Shay, *Achilles in Vietnam*, p. 98.
34. Quoted in Geoffrey C. Ward and Ken Burns, *The War: An Intimate History 1941–1945* (New York: Alfred A. Knopf, 2007), p. 391.
35. Filkins, *Forever War*, p. 198.
36. Ibid., p. 199.
37. Thomas, *The War Lovers*, p. 172.
38. William James, *The Varieties of Religious Experience* (New York: Modern Library, 1902/1929), p. 359.
39. Ibid., p. 358.
40. Ibid., p. 359.

4. PATRIOTISM

1. Jared Diamond, *Guns, Germs, and Steel* (New York: W. W. Norton, 2005), p. 278.
2. Eric Larson, *The Devil in the White City* (New York: Vintage Books, 2004), p. 181. See also the account in Susan Jacoby, *Freethinkers* (New York: Metropolitan Books, 2004), pp. 286–287.
3. Quoted in Russell Shorto, "Founding Father?" *The New York Times Magazine*, February 14, 2010: 39.
4. Quoted in Herbert Kliebard, *The Struggle for the American Curriculum* (New York: Routledge, 1995), p. 177. For accounts of similar reactions today, see Joel Westheimer, ed., *Pledging Allegiance: The Politics of Patriotism in America's Schools* (New York: Teachers College Press, 2007).
5. Martha C. Nussbaum, *For Love of Country?* ed. Joshua Cohen (Boston: Beacon Press, 1996), p. xi.
6. James Terry White, *Character Lessons in American Biography* (New York: The Character Development League, 1909), p. 96.
7. Ibid., p. 97.
8. Ibid.
9. Ibid., p. 101.
10. Nussbaum, *For Love of Country?*, p. 4. For a useful review of the literature on cosmopolitanism, see David T. Hansen, "Chasing Butterflies Without a Net: Interpreting Cosmopolitanism," *Studies in Philosophy of Education* 29, 2010: 151–166.
11. Thomas Paine, from the Preface to *The Age of Reason*. Quoted in Michael True, *An Energy Field More Intense Than War* (Syracuse, NY: Syracuse University Press, 1995), p. 14.
12. Quoted in ibid., p. 14.
13. Nussbaum, *For Love of Country?*, p. 5.
14. Ibid.
15. Quoted in Nicholson Baker, *Human Smoke: The Beginnings of World War II, the End of Civilization* (New York: Simon & Schuster, 2008), p. 286.
16. Benjamin Barber, "Constitutional Faith," in Nussbaum, *For Love of Country?*, p. 34.

17. Ibid., p. 33.
18. See Nel Noddings, *The Maternal Factor: Two Paths to Morality* (Berkeley: University of California Press, 2010).
19. Quoted in Baker, *Human Smoke*, p. 3.
20. Nussbaum, *For Love of Country?*, p. 15.
21. Barber, "Constitutional Faith," p. 36.
22. Jean Bethke Elshtain, *Women and War* (New York: Basic Books, 1987), p. 252.
23. Ibid., pp. 252–253.
24. David Tyack, *Seeking Common Ground: Public Schools in a Diverse Society* (Cambridge, MA: Harvard University Press, 2003), p. 48.
25. See Margaret S. Crocco and O. L. Davis, eds., *"Bending the Future to Their Will"* (Lanham, MD: Rowman & Littlefield, 1999); see also Linda Kerber, *Toward an Intellectual History of Women* (Chapel Hill: University of North Carolina Press, 1997).
26. See Kliebard, *Struggle for the American Curriculum*, pp. 172–176.
27. See, for example, the debate over whether the United States was founded as a Christian nation in Shorto, "Founding Father?," pp. 32–39, 46–47.
28. Ibid., p. 34.
29. Barbara W. Tuchman, *The March of Folly* (New York: Ballantine Books, 1984), p. 18.
30. Katherine Platt, "Places of Experience and the Experience of Place," in *The Longing for Home*, ed. Leroy S. Rouner (Notre Dame, IN: University of Notre Dame Press, 1996), p. 125.

5. HATRED

1. Quoted in Nicholson Baker, *Human Smoke: The Beginnings of World War II, the End of Civilization* (New York: Simon & Schuster, 2008), p. 449.
2. Robert Graves, *Goodbye to All That* (London: Folio Society, 1929/1981), p. 199.
3. Quoted in Andrew Fiala, *The Just War Myth* (Lanham, MD: Rowman & Littlefield, 2008), p. 50. The Hegel quotes are from Georg Hegel, *Philosophy of Right*, sec. 338, addition, 370 (Cambridge: Cambridge University Press, 1991).
4. Evan Thomas, *The War Lovers: Roosevelt, Lodge, Hearst, and the Rush to Empire, 1898* (New York: Little, Brown, 2010), p. 405.
5. Graves, *Goodbye to All That*, p. 208.
6. Sebastian Faulks, *Birdsong* (London: Vintage Books, 1988), pp. 482–483.
7. Quoted in Jonathan Glover, *Humanity: A Moral History of the Twentieth Century* (New Haven, CT: Yale University Press, 2000), p. 175.
8. Peter Schrijvers, *The GI War Against Japan* (New York: New York University Press, 2002), p. 208.
9. Quoted in Glover, *Humanity*, p. 175.

10. For detailed accounts, see Jonathan Shay, *Achilles in Vietnam: Combat Trauma and the Undoing of Character* (New York: Scribner, 1994).
11. See James Gilligan, *Violence* (New York: G. P. Putnam's Sons, 1996).
12. Some of these people appear in the account given by Anthony Swofford, *Jarhead* (New York: Scribner, 2003). See also Dexter Filkins, *The Forever War* (New York: Alfred A. Knopf, 2008).
13. J. G. Gray also discusses such men. J. G. Gray, *The Warriors: Reflections on Men in Battle* (Lincoln: University of Nebraska Press, 1959 and 1970).
14. Norman M. Naimark, *Fires of Hatred: Ethnic Cleansing in Twentieth-Century Europe* (Cambridge, MA: Harvard University Press, 2002), p. 6.
15. See Jan Gross, *Neighbors* (New York: Penguin Group, 2002). See also the comments in Robert Wistrich, *A Lethal Obsession: Anti-Semitism from Antiquity to the Global Jihad* (New York: Random House, 2010).
16. Quoted in Gross, *Neighbors*, p. 18.
17. Ibid., p. 97.
18. Ibid., pp. 95–96.
19. See Gilligan, *Violence*; also see Willard Gaylin, *Hatred: The Psychological Descent into Violence* (New York: Public Affairs, 2003).
20. Gaylin, *Hatred*, p. 2.
21. Gross, *Neighbors*, p. 105.
22. See again Gross, *Neighbors*. For an account of heroic people who saved the lives of their neighbors, see Samuel P. Oliner and Pearl M. Oliner, *The Altruistic Personality: Rescuers of Jews in Nazi Europe* (New York: Free Press, 1988).
23. See the chapter on Rwanda in Glover, *Humanity*.
24. Ibid., p. 121.
25. See Nel Noddings, *Critical Lessons: What Our Schools Should Teach* (Cambridge: Cambridge University Press, 2006).
26. Edward S. Casey, *Getting Back into Place* (Bloomington: Indiana University Press, 1993), p. 144.
27. Quoted in Naimark, *Fires of Hatred*, p. 110.
28. Ibid., p. 136.
29. Wistrich, *Lethal Obsession*, p. 928.
30. Louise Richardson, *What Terrorists Want: Understanding the Enemy, Containing the Threat* (New York: Random House, 2006), p. 176.
31. See Michael Bonner, *Jihad in Islamic History: Doctrines and Practice* (Princeton, NJ: Princeton University Press, 2006).
32. Richardson, *What Terrorists Want*, p. 177.
33. Mark Juergensmeyer, *Terror in the Mind of God: The Global Rise of Religious Violence* (Berkeley: University of California Press, 2000), p. 155.
34. Quoted in Richardson, *What Terrorists Want*, p. 222.
35. Ibid., p. 219.
36. Ibid.
37. Quoted in ibid., p. 220.
38. See Noddings, *Critical Lessons*; also see Noddings, *Happiness and Education* (Cambridge: Cambridge University Press, 2003).

## 6. RELIGION

1. Nel Noddings, *Educating for Intelligent Belief or Unbelief* (New York: Teachers College Press, 1993).
2. Ibid., p. xiii.
3. All quotes are from Daniel Bentley Hart, *Atheist Delusions: The Christian Revolution and Its Enemies* (New Haven, CT: Yale University Press, 2010), p. 4.
4. Ibid., p. xiii.
5. Ibid., p. 220.
6. Terry Eagleton, *Reason, Faith, and Revolution: Reflections on the God Debate* (New Haven, CT: Yale University Press, 2010), pp. 90–91.
7. Ibid., pp. 7–8; Paul Tillich, *The Courage to Be* (New Haven, CT: Yale University Pres, 1952); John Dewey, *A Common Faith, Later Works*, vol. 9: 1933–1934 (Carbondale: Southern Illinois Press, 1989), p. 34.
8. Eagleton, *Reason, Faith, and Revolution*, p. 168.
9. Edward O. Wilson, *The Creation: An Appeal to Save Life on Earth* (New York: W. W. Norton, 2006), p. 4.
10. Christopher Hitchens, *God is not Great: How Religion Poisons Everything* (New York: Twelve [Warner Books], 2007), p. 103.
11. Quoted in Janet Browne, *Charles Darwin: The Power of Place* (New York: Alfred A. Knopf, 2002), p. 432.
12. James Turner, *Without God, Without Creed* (Baltimore: Johns Hopkins University Press, 1985), p. 207.
13. Quoted in Jack Miles, *God: A Biography* (New York: Alfred A. Knopf, 1995), p. 309.
14. See Fyodor Dostoevsky, *The Brothers Karamazov*, trans. Constance Garnett (New York: Modern Library, n.d.).
15. Quoted in Turner, *Without God, Without Creed*, p. 207.
16. See Jared Diamond, *Guns, Germs, and Steel* (New York: W. W. Norton, 2005), p. 277.
17. Drew Gilpin Faust, *This Republic of Suffering: Death and the American Civil War* (New York: Alfred A. Knopf, 2008), p. 175.
18. Jack Miles, *Christ: A Crisis in the Life of God* (New York: Alfred A. Knopf, 2001), p. 200.
19. For a pictorial summary of these awful events, see James A. Haught, *Holy Horrors* (Buffalo: Prometheus Books, 1990). For a discussion of the persecution of women, see Mary Daly, *Beyond God the Father* (Boston: Beacon Press, 1974).
20. Michael K. Jerryson and Mark Juergensmeyer, eds., *Buddhist Warfare* (Oxford: Oxford University Press, 2010), p. 9.
21. Hitchens, *God is not Great*, chapter 14.
22. Hart, *Atheist Delusions*, p. 92.
23. Ibid., p. 91.
24. Bertrand Russell, *Why I Am Not a Christian* (New York: Simon and Schuster, 1957), p. 206.

25. See Deuteronomy 20.
26. Evan Thomas, *The War Lovers: Roosevelt, Lodge, Hearst, and the Rush to Empire, 1898* (New York: Little, Brown, 2010), p. 372.
27. Tillich, *The Courage to Be*, p. 190.
28. Martin Buber, *I and Thou*, trans. Walter Kaufmann (New York: Charles Scribner's Sons, 1970), p. 100.
29. Dewey, *A Common Faith*, p. 23.
30. Ibid., p. 34.
31. Nel Noddings, "Looking Forward from *A Common Faith*," in *John Dewey at 150*, ed. A. G. Rud, Jim Garrison, and Lynda Stone (West Lafayette, IN: Purdue University Press, 2009), pp. 11–17.
32. See Nel Noddings, *Women and Evil* (Berkeley: University of California Press, 1989).
33. Quoted in John Hick, *Evil and the God of Love* (New York: Macmillan, 1977), p. 159.
34. See C. S. Lewis, *The Problem of Pain* (New York: Macmillan, 1962); also see Lewis, *A Grief Observed* (Toronto: Bantam, 1976).
35. For a brief history of the preemptive war concept and a critique of its use in the Iraq war, see Andrew Fiala, *The Just War Myth* (Lanham, MD: Rowman & Littelfield, 2008).
36. Russell, *Why I Am Not a Christian*, p. 47.
37. Hick, *Evil and the God of Love*, p. 29.
38. I have argued this in several places. See, for example, Noddings, *Critical Lessons: What Our Schools Should Teach* (Cambridge: Cambridge University Press, 2006).

### 7. PACIFISM

1. See Christian Smith, *Soul Searching: The Religious and Spiritual Lives of American Teenagers* (Oxford: Oxford University Press, 2005).
2. Jonathan Glover, *Humanity: A Moral History of the Twentieth Century* (New Haven, CT: Yale University Press, 2000), chapter 40.
3. Ibid., p. 405.
4. On care ethics, see Virginia Held, *The Ethics of Care: Personal, Political, and Global* (Oxford: Oxford University Press, 2006); Nel Noddings, *The Maternal Factor: Two Paths to Morality* (Berkeley: University of California Press, 2010); Sara Ruddick, *Maternal Thinking: Toward a Politics of Peace* (Boston: Beacon Press, 1989); Michael Slote, *The Ethics of Care and Empathy* (New York: Routledge, 2007).
5. See John Howard Yoder, *The Politics of Jesus* (Grand Rapids, MI: Eerdmans, 1994).
6. See David Cortright, *Peace: A History of Movements and Ideas* (Cambridge: Cambridge University Press, 2008).
7. See Michael True, *An Energy Field More Intense Than War* (Syracuse, NY: Syracuse University Press, 1995).

8. Dorothy Day, *The Long Loneliness* (San Francisco: Harper & Row, 1952), p. 263.

9. Ibid., p. 264.

10. Ibid., p. 272.

11. Quoted in Daniel R. Smock, *Religious Perspectives on War* (Washington, DC: United States Institute of Peace Press, 1992), p. 17.

12. Nicholas D. Kristof, "In Israel, the Noble Vs. the Ugly," *New York Times*, July 8, 2010: A25.

13. Smock, *Religious Perspectives*, p. 23.

14. See Michael Bonner, *Jihad in Islamic History: Doctrines and Practice* (Princeton, NJ: Princeton University Press, 2006).

15. Ibid., p. 5.

16. David W. Chappell, ed., *Buddhist Peacework: Creating Cultures of Peace* (Boston: Wisdom Publications, 1999), p. 16.

17. See Daisaku Ikeda, *For the Sake of Peace: Seven Paths to Global Harmony* (Santa Monica, CA: Middleway Press, 2001); also see Daniel L. Smith-Christopher, ed., *Subverting Hatred: The Challenge of Nonviolence in Religious Traditions* (Maryknoll, NY: Orbis Books, 2002).

18. See Michael K. Jerryson and Mark Juergensmeyer, eds., *Buddhist Warfare* (Oxford: Oxford University Press, 2010).

19. See Barbara Wien, ed., *Peace and World Order Studies: A Curriculum Guide* (New York: World Policy Institute, 1984).

20. Cortright, *Peace*, p. 3.

21. Ibid., p. 5. Cortright cites Lotta Harbom, Stina Hogbladh, and Peter Wallensteen, "Armed Conflict and Peace Agreements," *Journal of Peace Research* 43(5), 2006: 617–631.

22. Cortright, *Peace*, p. 123.

23. Ibid., p. 172.

24. Quoted in ibid., p. 173.

25. Ibid., p. 176.

26. Quoted in ibid., p. 72.

27. This is a point made by Romain Rolland, quoted in ibid., p. 72.

28. For a history of conscientious objection, see Charles C. Moskos and John Whiteclay Chambers II, eds., *The New Conscientious Objection* (Oxford: Oxford University Press, 1993).

29. Jeff McMahan, *Killing in War* (Oxford: Clarendon Press, 2009).

30. For a discussion of contingent pacifism and conscientious refusal, see John Rawls, *A Theory of Justice* (Cambridge, MA: Harvard University Press, 1971), pp. 368–391. For further discussion of the varieties of pacifism, see Andrew Fiala, *The Just War Myth* (Lanham, MD: Rowman & Littlefield, 2008).

31. Robert B. Westbrook, *John Dewey and American Democracy* (Ithaca, NY: Cornell University Press, 1991), p. 205.

32. See Charles Howlett, "John Dewey and Peace Education," in Monisha Bajaj, ed., *Encyclopedia of Peace Education* (Charlotte, NC: Information Age, 2008), pp. 25–31.

33. Held, *Ethics of Care*, p. 160.
34. Noddings, *Maternal Factor*, p. 249.

## 8. WOMEN AND WAR

1. M. Esther Harding, *Woman's Mysteries* (New York: Harper & Row, 1971), p. 81.
2. Ibid.
3. See, for example, Estella Lauter and Carol Schrier Rupprecht, eds., *Feminist Archetypal Theory* (Knoxville: University of Tennessee Press, 1985).
4. For a fuller discussion and references, see Nel Noddings, *The Maternal Factor: Two Paths to Morality* (Berkeley: University of California Press, 2010).
5. See Richard Wrangham and Dale Peterson, *Demonic Males: Apes and the Origins of Human Violence* (New York: Houghton Mifflin, 1996).
6. Laura Duhan Kaplan, "Woman Caretaker: An Archetype That Supports Patriarchal Militarism," *Hypatia* 9, 1994: 123.
7. Nel Noddings, *Caring: A Feminine Approach to Ethics and Moral Education* (Berkeley: University of California Press, 1984), p. 2.
8. See Sara Ruddick, *Maternal Thinking: Toward a Politics of Peace* (Boston: Beacon Press, 1989).
9. See the symposium on *Caring* in *Hypatia* 5(1), 1990: 101–126.
10. Kaplan, "Woman Caretaker," p. 123.
11. Virginia Woolf, *Three Guineas* (New York: Harcourt Brace, 1938/1966), p. 74.
12. Ibid., p. 75.
13. Ibid., p. 109.
14. Ibid., p. 143.
15. See the account in Jean Bethke Elshtain, *Jane Addams and the Dream of American Democracy* (New York: Basic Books, 2002).
16. Ibid., p. 215.
17. Woolf, *Three Guineas*, pp. 60–62.
18. Ibid., p. 22.
19. See the account in Frances H. Early, *A World Without WAR* (Syracuse, NY: Syracuse University Press, 1997); also see Birgit Brock-Utne, *Educating for Peace: A Feminist Perspective* (New York and Oxford: Pergamon Press, 1985).
20. Betty A. Reardon, *Sexism and the War System* (New York: Teachers College Press, 1985), p. 97.
21. Brock-Utne, *Educating for Peace*, p. 32.
22. See both Brock-Utne, *Educating for Peace*, and Reardon, *Sexism and the War System*.
23. See Norman M. Naimark, *Fires of Hatred: Ethnic Cleansing in Twentieth-Century Europe* (Cambridge, MA: Harvard University Press, 2002).

24. Elise Boulding, *One Small Plot of Heaven* (Wallingford, PA: Pendle Hill, 1989); also see Nel Noddings, *Starting at Home: Caring and Social Policy* (Berkeley: University of California Press, 2002).

25. Boulding, *One Small Plot of Heaven*, p. 205.

26. The name and acronym are attributed to W. B. Gallie. See Ruddick, *Maternal Thinking*, p. 178.

27. Ibid., p. 179.

28. Ibid., p. 180.

29. Ibid.

30. Ibid., p. 181.

31. Carol J. Adams, "Bringing Peace Home: A Feminist Philosophical Perspective on the Abuse of Women, Children, and Pet Animals," *Hypatia* 9(2), 1994: 63–84.

32. See Michael Pollan, *The Omnivore's Dilemma* (New York: Penguin Group, 2006).

33. Virginia Woolf, *To the Lighthouse* (New York: Harcourt Brace/Harvest, 1955).

34. Woolf, *Three Guineas*, p. 142.

35. Genesis 1:26.

36. Matthew Scully, *Dominion: The Power of Man, the Suffering of Animals, and the Call to Mercy* (New York: St. Martin's Press, 2002).

37. Ibid., p. 398, quoting Revelations 21:4.

38. See, for example, Christine Downing, *The Goddess* (New York: Crossroad, 1984); Naomi R. Goldenberg, *Changing of the Gods* (Boston: Beacon Press, 1979); Gerda Lerner, *The Creation of Patriarchy* (New York: Oxford University Press, 1986); and Merlin Stone, *When God Was a Woman* (New York: Dial Press, 1976).

39. Riane Eisler, *The Chalice and the Blade* (New York: HarperCollins, 1987), p. 94.

## 9. EXISTENTIAL MEANING

1. Paul Tillich, *The Courage to Be* (New Haven, CT: Yale University Press, 1952).

2. See Jean-Paul Sartre, *Being and Nothingness*, trans. Hazel E. Barnes (New York: Washington Square Press, 1956); also see Sartre, *Nausea*, trans. Lloyd Alexander (Norfolk, CT: New Directions, 1959).

3. See Martin Buber, *I and Thou*, trans. Walter Kaufmann (New York: Charles Scribner's Sons, 1970).

4. Isaiah Berlin, *Four Essays on Liberty* (Oxford: Oxford University Press, 1969), p. 135.

5. Viktor E. Frankl, *The Doctor and the Soul* (New York: Vintage Books, 1973), p. 111.

6. Nel Noddings, *Happiness and Education* (Cambridge: Cambridge University Press, 2003), p. 41.

7. B. F. Skinner, *Beyond Freedom and Dignity* (New York: Vintage Books, 1972), p. 12.
8. Eric Hoffer, *The True Believer* (New York: Harper & Row, 1951), p. 92.
9. Ibid., p. 24.
10. J. G. Gray, *The Warriors: Reflections on Men in Battle* (Lincoln: University of Nebraska Press, 1959 and 1970), p. 29.
11. Quoted in Drew Gilpin Faust, *This Republic of Suffering: Death and the American Civil War* (New York: Alfred A. Knopf, 2008), p. 271.
12. See Noddings, *Happiness and Education*.
13. Simone Weil, *Simone Weil Reader*, ed. George A. Panichas (Mt. Kisco, NY: Moyer Bell Ltd., 1977), p. 290.
14. Voltaire, *Candide* in *The Portable Voltaire*, ed. Ben Ray Redman (New York: Penguin Books, 1977), pp. 324–325.
15. J. G. Farrell, *The Singapore Grip* (New York: New York Review of Books, 2004), p. 284.
16. Willa Cather, *The Professor's House*, in *Later Novels* (New York: Library of America, 1990), p. 114.
17. Gaston Bachelard, *The Poetics of Space*, trans. Maria Jolas (New York: Orion Press, 1964).
18. Ibid., p. 67.
19. Wallace Stegner, *Angle of Repose* (New York: Penguin Books, 1971), p. 277.
20. Ibid., p. 278.
21. Elise Boulding, *One Small Plot of Heaven* (Wallingford, PA: Pendle Hill, 1989), p. 179.
22. Ibid., p. 204.
23. Quoting Jean Amery, W. G. Sebald, *On the Natural History of Destruction*, trans. Anthea Bell (New York: Random House, 2003), pp. 160–161.

## 10. THE CHALLENGE TO EDUCATION

1. See Alfred North Whitehead, *The Aims of Education* (New York: Free Press, 1929/1967).
2. See Cass R. Sunstein, *Going to Extremes: How Like Minds Unite and Divide* (New York: Oxford University Press, 2009).
3. David Cortright, *Peace: A History of Movements and Ideas* (Cambridge: Cambridge University Press, 2008), p. 123. See also Andrew J. Bachevich, *Washington Rules: America's Path to Permanent War* (New York: Metropolitan Books, 2010).
4. For a lovely example, see Karen J. Rusthoven, *Success in Education Through Peace, Healing, and Hope* (Minneapolis: Syren, 2007).
5. Two noteworthy sources: Ikeda Center for Peace, Learning, and Dialogue, Cambridge, Massachusetts; *Peace Research: The Canadian Journal of Peace and Conflict Studies*.
6. Ian Harris and Mary Lee Morrison, *Peace Education*, 2nd ed. (Jefferson, NC: McFarland, 2003), p. 39.

7. See Myles Horton, *The Long Haul* (with Judith Kohl and Herbert Kohl) (New York: Teachers College Press, 1998).
8. See Barbara Applebaum, "Is Teaching for Social Justice a 'Liberal Bias'?" *Teachers College Record* 111(2), 2009: 376–408. ID=15200.
9. Christopher R. Leahey, *Whitewashing War* (New York: Teachers College Press, 2010), p. 98.
10. See Nel Noddings, *Happiness and Education* (Cambridge: Cambridge University Press, 2003); also see Noddings, *Critical Lessons: What Our Schools Should Teach* (Cambridge: Cambridge University Press, 2006).
11. Quoted in Stephen Thornton, *Teaching Social Studies That Matters: Curricula for Active Learning* (New York: Teachers College Press, 2005), p. 12.
12. Lyn Macdonald, ed., Introduction, *Anthem for Doomed Youth* (London: Folio Society, 2000), p. xxii.
13. See Bachevich, *Washington Rules*, pp. 225–226.
14. Quoted in Paul Edwards, William Alston, and A. N. Prior, "Bertrand Arthur William Russell," *Encyclopedia of Philosophy*, vol. 7 (New York: Macmillan and Free Press, 1972), p. 236.
15. Bertrand Russell, *New Hopes for a Changing World* (London: George Allen & Unwin Ltd., 1951), p. 164.
16. Ibid., pp. 162–163.
17. Ibid., p. 163.
18. Ibid., pp. 73–74.
19. Paul Ricoeur, *The Symbolism of Evil* (Boston: Beacon Press, 1969), p. 235.
20. See Daniel J. Levitin, *The World in Six Songs* (New York: Penguin Books, 2008).
21. Ibid., p. 13.
22. Susan Sontag, *Regarding the Pain of Others* (New York: Farrar, Strauss, and Giroux, 2003), p. 8.
23. Jonathan Glover, *Humanity: A Moral History of the Twentieth Century* (New Haven, CT: Yale University Press, 2000), p. 414.
24. Edward O. Wilson, *The Creation: An Appeal to Save Life on Earth* (New York: W. W. Norton, 2006), p. 137.
25. Gordon S. Wood, "No Thanks for the Memories," *The New York Review of Books*, January 13, 2011: 42.
26. Ibid. The embedded quote is from Bernard Bailyn.
27. Michael Bess, *Choices Under Fire: Moral Dimensions of World War II* (New York: Alfred A. Knopf, 2006), p. 311.
28. David F. Noble, *A World Without Women* (Oxford: Oxford University Press, 1993), p. 241.
29. See Charles Dickens, *Hard Times* (Harmondsworth, England: Penguin Books Ltd., 1854/1982).
30. Miguel de Unamuno, *Tragic Sense of Life*, trans. J. E. Crawford Flitch (New York: Dover Books, 1954), p. 3.
31. On the psychology of national leaders, see Greg Cashman, *What Causes War?* (New York: Macmillan/Lexington, 1993).

# BIBLIOGRAPHY

Adams, Carol J. "Bringing Peace Home: A Feminist Philosophical Perspective on the Abuse of Women, Children, and Pet Animals," *Hypatia* 9(2), 1994: 63–84.

Applebaum, Barbara. "Is Teaching for Social Justice a 'Liberal Bias'?" *Teachers College Record*, 111(2), 2009: 376–408.

Bachelard, Gaston. *The Poetics of Space*, trans. Maria Jolas. New York: Orion Press, 1964.

Bachevich, Andrew J. *Washington Rules: America's Path to Permanent War*. New York: Metropolitan Books, 2010.

Baker, Nicholson. *Human Smoke: The Beginnings of World War II, the End of Civilization*. New York: Simon & Schuster, 2008.

Barber, Benjamin. "Constitutional Faith," in Nussbaum, *For Love of Country?* pp. 30–37.

Berlin, Isaiah. *Four Essays on Liberty*. Oxford: Oxford University Press, 1969.

Bess, Michael. *Choices Under Fire: Moral Dimensions of World War II*. New York: Alfred A. Knopf, 2006.

Bonner, Michael. *Jihad in Islamic History: Doctrines and Practice*. Princeton, NJ: Princeton University Press, 2006.

Boulding, Elise. *One Small Plot of Heaven*. Wallingford, PA: Pendle Hill, 1989.

Brock-Utne, Birgit. *Educating for Peace: A Feminist Perspective*. New York and Oxford: Pergamon Press, 1985.

Brooke, Rupert. "The Soldier," in Macdonald, *Anthem for Doomed Youth*.

Browne, Janet. *Charles Darwin: The Power of Place*. New York: Alfred A. Knopf, 2002.

Buber, Martin. *Pointing the Way*, trans. and ed. Maurice Friedman. New York: Harper & Row, 1957.

Buber, Martin. *I and Thou*, trans. Walter Kaufmann. New York: Charles Scribner's Sons, 1970.

Casey, Edward S. *Getting Back into Place*. Bloomington: Indiana University Press, 1993.

Cashman, Greg. *What Causes War?* New York: Macmillan/Lexington, 1993.

Cather, Willa. *The Professor's House* in *Later Novels*. New York: Library of America, 1990.

Chappell, David W., ed. *Buddhist Peacework: Creating Cultures of Peace*. Boston: Wisdom Publications, 1999.

Cortright, David. *Peace: A History of Movements and Ideas*. Cambridge: Cambridge University Press, 2008.

Crocco, Margaret S. and Davis, O. L., eds. *"Bending the Future to Their Will."* Lanham, MD: Rowman & Littlefield, 1999.

Daly, Mary. *Beyond God the Father*. Boston: Beacon Press, 1974.

Dawes, James. *The Language of War*. Cambridge, MA: Harvard University Press, 2002.

Day, Dorothy. *The Long Loneliness*. San Francisco: Harper & Row, 1952.

Derrida, Jacques. *Of Grammatology*, trans. Gayatri Chakravorty Spivak. Baltimore: Johns Hopkins University Press, 1976.

Dewey, John. *A Common Faith*, in *Later Works, vol. 9: 1933–1934*. Carbondale: Southern Illinois University Press, 1989.

Diamond, Jared. *Guns, Germs, and Steel*. New York: W. W. Norton, 2005.

Dickens, Charles. *Hard Times*. Harmondsworth, England: Penguin Books Ltd., 1854/1982.

Dostoevsky, Fyodor. *The Brothers Karamazov*, trans. Constance Garnett. New York: Modern Library, n.d.

Downing, Christine. *The Goddess*. New York: Crossroad, 1984.

Dugatkin, Lee Alan. *The Altruism Equation*. Princeton, NJ: Princeton University Press, 2006.

Eagleton, Terry. *Reason, Faith, and Revolution: Reflections on the God Debate*. New Haven, CT: Yale University Press, 2010.

Early, Frances H. *A World Without WAR*. Syracuse: Syracuse University Press, 1997.

Edwards, Paul, Alston, William, and Prior, A. N. "Bertrand Arthur William Russell," *Encyclopedia of Philosophy*, vol. 7. New York: Macmillan and the Free Press, 1972.

Eisler, Riane. *The Chalice and the Blade*. New York: HarperCollins, 1987.

Elshtain, Jean Bethke. *Women and War*. New York: Basic Books, 1987.

   *Jane Addams and the Dream of American Democracy*. New York: Basic Books, 2002.

Elshtain, Jean Bethke and Tobias, Sheila, eds. *Women, Militarism, and War*. Savage, MD: Rowman & Littlefield, 1990.

Farrell, J. G. *The Singapore Grip*. New York: New York Review of Books, 2004.

Faulks, Sebastian. *Birdsong*. London: Vintage Books, 1988.

Faust, Drew Gilpin. *This Republic of Suffering: Death and the American Civil War*. New York: Alfred A. Knopf, 2008.

Fiala, Andrew. *The Just War Myth*. Lanham, MD: Rowman & Littlefield, 2008.

Filkins, Dexter. *The Forever War.* New York: Alfred A. Knopf, 2008.

Frankl, Viktor E. *The Doctor and the Soul.* New York: Vintage Books, 1973.

Friedrich, Jorg. *The Fire: The Bombing of Germany 1940–1945.* New York: Columbia University Press, 2006.

Fukuyama, Francis. *The End of History and the Last Man.* New York: Free Press, 1992.

Gaylin, Willard. *Hatred: The Psychological Descent into Violence.* New York: Public Affairs, 2003.

Gilligan, James. *Violence.* New York: G. P. Putnam's Sons, 1996.

Glover, Jonathan. *Humanity: A Moral History of the Twentieth Century.* New Haven, CT: Yale University Press, 2000.

Goldenberg, Naomi R. *Changing of the Gods.* Boston: Beacon Press, 1979.

Goldensohn, Lorrie. *Dismantling Glory.* New York: Columbia University Press, 2003.

Graves, Robert. *Goodbye to All That.* London: Folio Society, 1929/1981.

Gray, J. G. *The Warriors: Reflections on Men in Battle.* Lincoln: University of Nebraska Press, 1959 and 1970.

Gross, Jan. *Neighbors.* New York: Penguin Group, 2002.

Hansen, David T. "Chasing Butterflies Without a Net: Interpreting Cosmopolitanism," *Studies in Philosophy of Education* 29, 2010: 151–166.

Harbom, Lotta, Hogbladh, Stina, and Wallensteen, Peter. "Armed Conflict and Peace Agreements," *Journal of Peace Research* 43(5), 2006: 617–631.

Harding, M. Esther. *Woman's Mysteries.* New York: Harper & Row, 1971.

Harris, Ian and Morrison, Mary Lee. *Peace Education,* 2nd ed. Jefferson, NC: McFarland, 2003.

Hart, Daniel Bentley. *Atheist Delusions: The Christian Revolution and Its Enemies.* New Haven, CT: Yale University Press, 2010.

Haught, James A. *Holy Horrors.* Buffalo, NY: Prometheus Books, 1990.

Hegel, Georg. *Philosophy of Right,* sec. 338, addition. Cambridge: Cambridge University Press, 1991.

Held, Virginia. *The Ethics of Care: Personal, Political, and Global.* Oxford: Oxford University Press, 2006.

Hick, John. *Evil and the God of Love.* New York: Macmillan, 1977.

Hitchens, Christopher. *God is not Great: How Religion Poisons Everything.* New York: Twelve [Warner Books], 2007.

Hoffer, Eric. *The True Believer.* New York: Harper & Row, 1951.

Horton, Miles. *The Long Haul,* with Judith Kohl and Herbert Kohl. New York: Teachers College Press, 1998.

Howlett, Charles. "John Dewey and Peace Education," in *Encyclopedia of Peace Education,* ed. Monisha Bajaj. Charlotte, NC: Information Age, 2008, pp. 25–31.

Huntington, Samuel P. *The Clash of Civilizations and the Remaking of World Order.* New York: Simon & Schuster, 1996.

Ikeda, Daisaku. *For the Sake of Peace: Seven Paths to Global Harmony.* Santa Monica, CA: Middleway Press, 2001.

Jacoby, Susan. *Freethinkers*. New York: Metropolitan Books, 2004.

James, William. *The Varieties of Religious Experience*. New York: Modern Library, 1902/1929.

Jerryson, Michael K. and Juergensmeyer, Mark, eds. *Buddhist Warfare*. Oxford: Oxford University Press, 2010.

Juergensmeyer, Mark. *Terror in the Mind of God: The Global Rise of Religious Violence*. Berkeley: University of California Press, 2000.

Jung, Carl G. *Answer to Job*, in *Collected Works*, vol. 2. Princeton, NJ: Princeton University Press, 1969.

Kagan, Robert. *The Return of History and the End of Dreams*. New York: Vintage Books, 2008.

Kaplan, Laura Duhan. "Woman Caretaker: An Archetype That Supports Patriarchal Militarism," *Hypatia* 9, 1994: 123–133.

Kerber, Linda. *Toward an Intellectual History of Women*. Chapel Hill: University of North Carolina Press, 1997.

Kimmel, Michael S. "Clarence, William, Iron Mike, Tailhook, Senator Packwood, Spur Posse, Magic … and Us," in *Transforming a Rape Culture*, ed. Emilie Buchwald, Pamela R. Fletcher, and Martha Roth. Minneapolis: Milkweed Editions, 1993, pp. 119–138

Kipling, Rudyard. "Tommy," in *Kipling: A Selection of His Stories and Poems*, vol. III, ed. John Beecroft. Garden City, NY: 1956, pp. 491–492.

Kliebard, Herbert. *The Struggle for the American Curriculum*. New York: Routledge, 1995.

Kristof, Nicholas D. "In Israel, the Noble Vs. the Ugly," *New York Times*, July 8, 2010: A25.

Larson, Eric. *The Devil in the White City*. New York: Vintage Books, 2004.

Lauter, Estella and Rupprecht, Carol Schrier, eds. *Feminist Archetypal Theory*. Knoxville: University of Tennessee Press, 1985.

Leahey, Christopher R. *Whitewashing War*. New York: Teachers College Press, 2010.

Lerner, Gerda. *The Creation of Patriarchy*. New York: Oxford University Press, 1986.

Levi, Primo. *The Drowned and the Saved*, trans. Raymond Rosenthal. New York: Vintage Books, 1988.

Levitin, Daniel J. *The World in Six Songs*. New York: Penguin Books, 2008.

Lewis, C. S. *The Problem of Pain*. New York: Macmillan, 1962.

*A Grief Observed*. Toronto: Bantam, 1976.

Macdonald, Lyn, ed. *Anthem for Doomed Youth*. London: Folio Society, 2000.

Massing, Michael. "The Volunteer Army: Who Fights and Why?" *New York Review of Books* 55 (April 3, 2008): 34–46.

McMahan, Jeff. *Killing in War*. Oxford: Clarendon Press, 2009.

Menand, Louis. *The Metaphysical Club*. New York: Farrar, Strauss and Giroux, 2001.

Miles, Jack. *God: A Biography*. New York: Alfred A. Knopf, 1995.

Miles, Jack. *Christ: A Crisis in the Life of God*. New York: Alfred A. Knopf, 2001.

Moskos, Charles C. and Chambers, John Whiteclay II, eds. *The New Conscientious Objection*. Oxford: Oxford University Press, 1993.

Mueller, John. *Retreat from Doomsday: The Obsolescence of War*. New York: Basic Books, 1989.

Naimark, Norman M. *Fires of Hatred: Ethnic Cleansing in Twentieth-Century Europe*. Cambridge, MA: Harvard University Press, 2002.

Noble, Daniel F. *A World Without Women*. Oxford: Oxford University Press, 1993.

Noddings, Nel. *Caring: A Feminine Approach to Ethics and Moral Education*. Berkeley: University of California Press, 1984.

*Women and Evil*. Berkeley: University of California Press, 1989.

*Educating for Intelligent Belief or Unbelief*. New York: Teachers College Press, 1993.

*Starting at Home: Caring and Social Policy*. Berkeley: University of California Press, 2002.

*Happiness and Education*. Cambridge: Cambridge University Press, 2003.

ed., *Educating Citizens for Global Awareness*. New York: Teachers College Press, 2005.

*Critical Lessons: What Our Schools Should Teach*. Cambridge: Cambridge University Press, 2006.

"Looking Forward from *A Common Faith*," in *John Dewey at 150*, ed. A. G. Rud, Jim Garrison, and Lynda Stone. West Lafayette, IN: Purdue University Press, 2009, pp. 11–17.

*The Maternal Factor: Two Paths to Morality*. Berkeley: University of California Press, 2010.

Nussbaum, Martha C. *For Love of Country?* ed. Joshua Cohen. Boston: Beacon Press, 1996.

O'Connell, Robert L. *Ride of the Second Horseman: The Birth and Death of War*. Oxford: Oxford University Press, 1995.

Okin, Susan Moller. *Women in Western Political Thought*. Princeton, NJ: Princeton University Press, 1979.

Oliner, Samuel P. and Oliner, Pearl M. *The Altruistic Personality: Rescuers of Jews in Nazi Europe*. New York: Free Press, 1988.

Owen, Wilfred. "Dulce et Decorum Est," in Macdonald, *Anthem for Dead Youth*.

Packer, George. "Embers," *The New Yorker*, February 1, 2010: 32–39.

Parsons, Susan Frank, ed. *The Cambridge Companion to Feminist Theology*. Cambridge: Cambridge University Press, 2002.

Phillips, J. Anthony. *Eve: The History of an Idea*. San Francisco: Harper & Row, 1984.

Plato. *The Republic of Plato*. Trans. with Notes and an "Interpretive Essay," Allan Bloom. New York: Basic Books, 1968.

Platt, Katherine. "Places of Experience and the Experience of Place," in *The Longing for Home*, ed. Leroy S. Rouner. Notre Dame, IN: University of Notre Dame Press, 1996, pp. 112–127.

Pollan, Michael. *The Omnivore's Dilemma*. New York: Penguin Group, 2006.

Rawls, John. *A Theory of Justice*. Cambridge, MA: Harvard University Press, 1971.

Reardon, Betty A. *Sexism and the War System*. New York: Teachers College Press, 1985.

Rich, Adrienne. *Of Woman Born*. New York: W. W. Norton, 1976.

Richardson, Louise. *What Terrorists Want: Understanding the Enemy, Containing the Threat*. New York: Random House, 2006.

Ricoeur, Paul. *The Symbolism of Evil*. Boston: Beacon Press, 1969.

Ruddick, Sara. *Maternal Thinking: Toward a Politics of Peace*. Boston: Beacon Press, 1989.

Russell, Bertrand. *New Hopes for a Changing World*. London: George Allen & Unwin Ltd., 1951.

*Why I Am Not a Christian*. New York: Simon and Schuster, 1957.

Rusthoven, Karen J. *Success in Education Through Peace, Healing, and Hope*. Minneapolis: Syren, 2007.

Sartre, Jean-Paul. *Being and Nothingness*, trans. Hazel E. Barnes. New York: Washington Square Press, 1956.

*Nausea*, trans. Lloyd Alexander. Norfolk, CT: New Directions, 1959.

Schein, Seth L. *The Mortal Hero*. Berkeley: University of California Press, 1984.

Schrijvers, Peter. *The GI War Against Japan*. New York: New York University Press, 2002.

Schwartz, Regina M. *The Curse of Cain: The Violent Legacy of Monotheism*. Chicago: University of Chicago Press, 1997.

Scully, Matthew. *Dominion: The Power of Man, the Suffering of Animals, and the Call to Mercy*. New York: St. Martin's Press, 2002.

Sebald, W. G. *On the Natural History of Destruction*, trans. Anthea Bell. New York: Random House, 2003.

Shay, Jonathan. *Achilles in Vietnam: Combat Trauma and the Undoing of Character*. New York: Scribner, 1994.

Shorto, Russell. "Founding Father?" *New York Times Magazine*. February 14, 2010: 32–39, 46–47.

Skinner, B. F. *Beyond Freedom and Dignity*. New York: Vintage Books, 1972.

Slote, Michael. *The Ethics of Care and Empathy*. New York: Routledge, 2007.

Smith, Christian. *Soul Searching: The Religious and Spiritual Lives of Teenagers*. Oxford: Oxford University Press, 2005.

Smith-Christopher, Daniel L., ed. *Subverting Hatred: The Challenge of Nonviolence in Religious Traditions*. Maryknoll, NY: Orbis Books, 2002.

Smock, Daniel R. *Religious Perspectives on War*. Washington, DC: United States Institute of Peace Press, 1992.

Sontag, Susan. "Looking at War," *The New Yorker*, December 9, 2002: 82–98.

*Regarding the Pain of Others*. New York: Farrar, Straus, and Giroux, 2003.

Stegner, Wallace. *Angle of Repose*. New York: Penguin Books, 1971.

Stone, Merlin. *When God Was a Woman*. New York: Dial Press, 1976.

Sunstein, Cass R. *Going to Extremes: How Like Minds Unite and Divide*. New York: Oxford University Press, 2009.

Swofford, Anthony. *Jarhead*. New York: Scribner, 2003.

Tatum, James. *The Mourner's Song*. Chicago: University of Chicago Press, 2004.

Thomas, Evan. *The War Lovers: Roosevelt, Lodge, Hearst, and the Rush to Empire, 1898*. New York: Little Brown, 2010.

Thornton, Stephen. *Teaching Social Studies That Matters: Curricula for Active Learning*. New York: Teachers College Press, 2005.

Tillich, Paul. *The Courage To Be*. New Haven, CT: Yale University Press, 1952.

True, Michael. *An Energy Field More Intense Than War*. Syracuse, NY: Syracuse University Press, 1995.

Tuchman, Barbara W. *The March of Folly*. New York: Ballantine Books, 1984.

Turner, James. *Without God, Without Creed*. Baltimore: Johns Hopkins University Press, 1985.

Tyack, David. *Common Ground: Public Schools in a Diverse Society*. Cambridge, MA: Harvard University Press, 2003.

Unamuno, Miguel de. *Tragic Sense of Life*, trans. J. E. Crawford Flitch. New York: Dover Books, 1954.

Voltaire. *Candide*, in *The Portable Voltaire*, ed. Ben Ray Redman. New York: Penguin Books, 1977.

Walzer, Michael. *Just and Unjust Wars*. New York: Basic Books, 1977.

Ward, Geoffrey C. and Burns, Ken. *The War: An Intimate History 1941–1945*. New York: Alfred A. Knopf, 2007.

Weil, Simone. "The *Iliad*, Poem of Might," in *Simone Weil Reader*, ed. George A. Panichas. Mt. Kisco, NY: Moyer Bell Ltd., 1977, pp. 153–183.

Westbrook, Robert B. *John Dewey and American Democracy*. Ithaca, NY: Cornell University Press, 1991.

Westheimer, Joel, ed. *Pledging Allegiance: The Politics of Patriotism in America's Schools*. New York: Teachers College Press, 2007.

White, James Terry. *Character Lessons in American Biography*. New York: The Character Development League, 1909.

Whitehead, Alfred North. *The Aims of Education*. New York: Free Press, 1929/1967.

Wien, Barbara, ed. *Peace and World Order Studies: A Curriculum Guide*. New York: World Policy Institute, 1984.

Wilson, Edward O. *The Creation: An Appeal to Save Life on Earth*. New York: W. W. Norton, 2006.

Wissler, Clark. *Indians of the United States*. New York: Anchor Books, 1989.

Wistrich, Robert. *A Lethal Obsession: Anti-Semitism from Antiquity to the Global Jihad*. New York: Random House, 2010.

Wood, Gordon S. "No Thanks for the Memories," *The New York Review of Books*, January 13, 2011.

Woolf, Virginia. *Three Guineas*. New York: Harcourt Brace, 1938/1966.

   *To the Lighthouse*. New York: Harcourt Brace/Harvest, 1955.

Wrangham, Richard and Peterson, Dale. *Demonic Males: Apes and the Origins of Human Violence*. New York: Houghton Mifflin, 1996.

Yoder, John Howard. *The Politics of Jesus*. Grand Rapids, MI: Eerdmans, 1994.

# INDEX